NEW YORK FIREFIGHTING
AND THE
AMERICAN REVOLUTION

NEW YORK
FIREFIGHTING
— AND THE —
American Revolution

SAVING COLONIAL GOTHAM FROM INCINERATION

BRUCE TWICKLER

THE
History
PRESS

Published by The History Press
Charleston, SC
www.historypress.com

Back cover: *General George Washington at Trenton,* by John Trumball, Philadelphia, 1792. *Courtesy of Yale University Art Gallery.*

Other cover illustrations are courtesy of Docema LLC.

First published 2022

Manufactured in the United States

ISBN 9781467150859

Library of Congress Control Number: 2022930153

To the memory of my eighth-grade history teacher,
Edward Adair, and my father, George Twickler,
both of whom inspired my passion for history.

CONTENTS

ACKNOWLEDGEMENTS

$\mathcal{N}$o book is an island, as John Donne's publisher used to say, and the beginning, middle and end of this book are connected to the "main" by three scholars who embody accurate and rigorous research—Jaap Jacobs, Jill Lepore and Benjamin Carp. Jaap convinced me that the "received views" of Stuyvesant being a tyrant were overdrawn. Professor Lepore directed me to her online database of the coordinates of the fires of 1741, a most admirable depth of detail we used for our map of the fires. Ben published solid evidence that, contrary to historical opinion, the New York fire in 1776 was more deliberate than accidental—evidence I found persuasive.

Frank Fox provided me with the list of the specific armament of the English ships for the mission to seize Manhattan from the Dutch. He did consult a refence he had at hand, but I would not have blinked if he had told me from memory. Richard Howe favored me by reading an early version of the manuscript. His meticulous estimate of the number of buildings destroyed in the 1776 fire as it appeared in the *Gotham Blog* inspired me to be as thorough. The editor at the *Gotham Blog*, Robb Haberman, managed the review of my article on the Carleton Commission, much to the benefit of the article and its subsequent rendering in this book.

We relied on Jeroen van den Hurk's scholarship and drawings to build our 3D computer model of the Roelantsen House. We also used his work as the basis for several of the buildings of Dutch Manhattan as seen in the film *Broadside* and the views illustrated in this book. I would like to thank

Erik Sanderson and his Mannahatta Project for the topographical data used for the landscapes in both *Broadside* and this book. I also benefited from discussions with Ila Malloy, who, along with the Stoutenburgh family tree website, enabled me to keep track of the many "Isaac" and "Jacobus" family members across several generations.

I am very grateful to the New-York Historical Society and its cordial, knowledgeable and proficient staff members who unearthed maps, illustrations and the seminal Carleton Commission Report during my visits over the last several years. I also want to thank the people at the New York Public Library and the City Museum of New York for their invaluable help over the years and especially during this project. A special thanks goes to Gary Urbanowitz at the New York City Fire Museum for his encouragement, support and access to the extraordinary original manuscript of the British appointment of the five Loyalist firefighters to manage the FDNY during the Revolution.

Several professional reviewers influenced the progress and scope of this book. Esmond Harmsworth, the president of Aevitas, reviewed an early version of the manuscript and offered invaluable advice for possible paths to publishing. Robert Kaiser, the former managing editor of the *Washington Post*, also reviewed an early version of this book and candidly projected what to expect from publishers: "Editors at publishers edit; that's what they do—edit. Do not be surprised when they do it." The in-depth, comprehensive and encouraging reviews of later drafts of the book from experienced and skilled professional editors—Chad Rhoad in the United States and Trevor Anderson in the United Kingdom, added momentum to the project.

My friends and brothers James Monk, Kevin Holian and Eric Twickler read sections of the book as they were being written and suggested corrections and clarifications. Notably, Doug McCraith, while plowing through an early narrative of the 1776 fire, remarked, "I sure could use a map here." A special thanks to Barry Gerken, who read all three versions of the manuscript and, for each version, made valuable suggestions and corrections. He has the distinction of being the only person in the world who will ever correct the endnotes section three times.

Acknowledgements in the category "without whom this book could not have been published" must include Banks Smither, our acquisition editor at History Press, and Devan Calabrez, my friend and colleague. Banks guided this first-time effort along the yellow-brick road of publishing. He provided informed counsel, professional direction and timely support. Devan built our website and populated it with a host of original videos, animations, models, maps and illustrations. More than just contributing his many talents, Devan was my essential collaborator for every facet of the project, giving the book a third dimension, at least—if not a fourth.

And most importantly, my love and gratitude go to my wife, Janet Holian, who encouraged, supported, endured and promoted this project from its inception.

INTRODUCTION

NEW YORK FIREFIGHTING
AND THE AMERICAN REVOLUTION

a history of the colonial fire department in the city of New York, particularly its role in the American Revolution, is long overdue. Our story begins with the people of New York in the city's first century, as they fought fires, saved lives and protected their homes and livelihoods. Among those people were a group of volunteers, unpaid, who were the thin leather line, the colonial FDNY (Fire Department of New York), that stood between New York and disaster during periods of rampant arson, wars for North America and the American Revolution.

As the volunteers of the fire department were not among the famous elite, their story during the war years has been neglected. The firefighters in this book were ordinary people—carpenters and coopers, blacksmiths and bakers—embroiled in confusing and violent times. They, like every New Yorker, were forced to make life-altering decisions when the opposing armies descended on the city early in the Revolution and the shooting started.

This narrative adds a new dimension to the understanding of this turbulent colonial period. It describes the motivation of the colonial legislature to buy fire engines and then create a fire department in the late 1730s. It also tracks the rapid growth of the department, funded by the wealth from the mid-century's Anglo-French wars. Finally, it examines the political pressures on firefighters throughout the Revolutionary period. The story, complementing other recent research, also dispels many of the myths about colonial firefighting propagated in histories since the Revolution.

Although overdue, it is probably true that even a decade ago, the narrative could not be told as it is here. For example, it is hard to evaluate the colonial fire department in New York unless you know something about the size and frequency of colonial fires. There has been a record of these fires for a few centuries, but they were buried in the newspapers of the time. Why hadn't anyone, a brave historian or zealous PhD candidate, resurrected them? The answer to that question is microfiche.

In the olden days, long forgotten—say before 2008—to read old newspapers, you had to go to the library, get the rolls of film that you wanted and put them into a torture machine, which was called the microfiche reader. Then you would read them on this dim viewer—in this case, thirty years of daily newspapers between 1750 to 1780—until either your eyes or your brain (sometimes both) no longer functioned.

Luckily, by 2014, at the start of this project, the digitization revolution was happening. Colonial newspapers were digitized, every colonial document was readable online and lists of the loyalists and military in the Revolution were one click away—the vast archive of history delivered to your laptop. It took little time and virtually no health risk to compile the data seen in the graph *Newsworthy Fires in New York (1766–1775)*.

Even more, if you want to read about the severity of any specific fire in that period, there is a direct link to the original newspaper article on the Saving New York: New York Firefighting & the American Revolution website (savingny.com). The fire data, when correlated with the growth

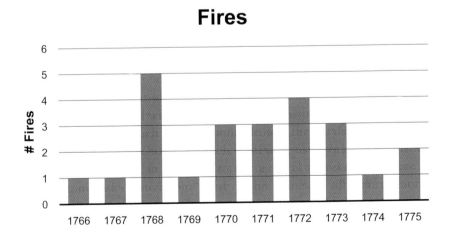

Newsworthy Fires (1766–1775).

of the department culled from the online city council records, underlines the influence of politics on the colonial fire department. Often, the understandable political response in years of bad fires was more engines and more firefighters.

Our political story continues as it follows the fire department through the confusing flux of civil governance from 1774 through 1776. The soon-to-be-feckless colonial provincial assembly regarded the fire department it had created as a bulwark against the dangers of conflagration. In contrast, when the newly-in-charge Patriot committees, like the Committee of Safety, looked at the fire department, they saw a battalion of recruits suitable to incorporate into Washington's Continental army or the state militia. Soon, even before the Revolution came to New York, every firefighter had to make a life-altering choice—join the military, get out of town or assume a low-profile existence and hope the whole thing would blow over.

Of course, the whole thing did not blow over. The maelstrom fell on New York in mid-1776 with a large British expeditionary force, thirty thousand troops, bulking up on Staten Island. The British would soon confront George Washington and his army, who were fortifying Manhattan and Long Island. After pushing Washington off Long Island, the British attacked across the East River in a massive amphibious operation that forced Washington to retreat north to the heights of Harlem.

Shortly after midnight on September 21, 1776, several fires erupted in lower Manhattan. By daybreak, they had consumed five hundred buildings, the most destructive fire in colonial North America.[1] The timing of the fires was suspicious. British troops had been in the city for only a few days after forcing Washington's army north. Were the fires accidental, deliberate arson or both? Why did the fire spread so quickly? Where were the firefighters?

Extinguishing fires in the eighteenth century depended on firefighters, engines and bucket brigades, a line of colonists passing water buckets to fill the fire engines. As it happened, by the third week of September 1776, every crucial component of the city's firefighting was compromised. Jacobus Stoutenburgh, the fire chief, and many other firefighters who were committed to the Revolution left the city when Washington moved north. Twenty thousand people, 80 percent of the city's prewar populace, had fled the conflict as it came closer, which decimated the bucket brigades.[2] Revolutionary vandals disabled pumps and cut holes in buckets.[3] Considering the diaspora of citizens and firemen, the havoc from a score of alleged arsonists and actual vandals and a stiff wind from the south, the city was fortunate to lose only 15 to 20 percent of its buildings.[4]

The narrative of the 1776 fire presented in this book is told from a firefighting perspective and includes the crucial actions of the New York firefighters, those who were still in the city that night. As bad as it was—and it was horrific—there were boundaries defended that the fire did not cross. Somebody fought that fire. The detailed street-by-street maps with the narrative demonstrate the opportunities lost and the hard-fought wins.

There is some historical controversy over the cause of and culpability for the fire. Many historians believe it to be accidental, with no clear evidence of deliberate arson.[5] Others point to growing evidence that although the original blaze may have been accidental, it was aided and abetted by people who were unsympathetic to the British occupation of New York. Luckily, to help you decide, this book presents an investigation that analyzes the controversy in the context of the Carleton Commission.[6]

The Carleton manuscript has sworn testimony from almost forty eyewitnesses, evidence rarely seen and not easily available until transcribed and placed online on the Saving New York website in 2016. Even better, if you are disinclined to read the entire report, you can get the gist of it by simply glancing at the map titled *Explosives Discovered at the 1776 Fire*. Each number on the map represents an explosive, such as a fused barrel of gunpowder or a bundle of flammable firesticks. These unexploded firebombs, discovered during and after the fire, were evidence of something—if not deliberate arson, perhaps the hope of deliberate arson.

While the cause and responsibility for the 1776 fire are controversial, few historians refer to or even have opinions about the role of the fire department from 1776 through 1783, the years of the Revolutionary War. It is this vacuum that this book's narrative fills. One or two historians do portray the department at the end of the war as decrepit, a shadow of its former self.[7] This is one of the myths addressed and corrected in this narrative.

For example, one historian claimed that there was only one fire engine operable at the end of the war. He was misinformed. There was no shortage of fire engines at the end of the war. The five Loyalist engineers who were managing the FDNY, veteran foremen of fire companies, all could maintain and repair engines. One of them, George Stanton, even built three of the engines before the war. Municipal lotteries ensured the fire department was well funded. It even had enough for the addition of at least two engines during the war.[8] In the end, as described later, it is the clear record of the fires successfully fought during the war that tells the real story.[9]

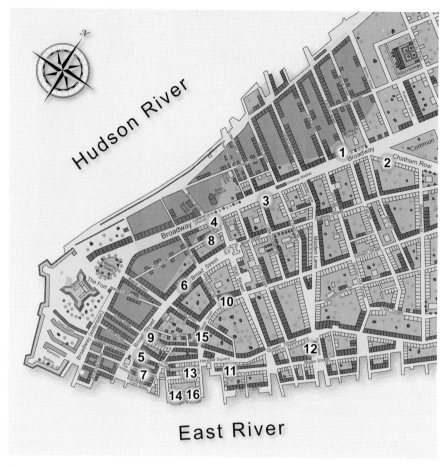

Explosives Discovered at the 1776 Fire.

The Saving New York Project has two major components—the *New York Firefighting* book and the appendix on the website at https://www.savingny. com/appendices1.html. The book contains the narrative, the story of the colonial fire department from its origins through Revolutionary victory. It also has many original illustrations, including maps and models that clarify potentially complex subjects, such as the 1776 fire or the Newsham fire engine.[10]

The appendices enable history buffs and students to easily dig deeper into the history, for example, by clicking the thumbnail links to the articles on fires in colonial newspapers or browsing the expanded views of the Newsham engine, including the intricacy of its inner works. Scholars may value the spreadsheet databases generated from lists in references, such as the 1703 census or the comprehensive list of Loyalists. All scholars, students and buffs now have access to the Carleton Commission, an important Revolutionary document. They are invited to improve the interpretation and/or transcription on the website.

Since this book is largely a story about choices, individual decisions, collective social preferences and the mandates of political will, it can perhaps provide relevant insights for today. Must we have a disaster to muster the political will to do what we should have done before it happened? In the case of the colonial history of the fire department, sometimes we got it right, sometimes we got it wrong and sometimes, when all hell broke loose, it was time to assume a low profile.

Part One

ORIGIN OF THE COLONIAL FIRE DEPARTMENT OF NEW YORK (1640–1740)

Mill near the fort in Manhattan (circa 1665)—cutting wood for the wooden city.

1

STUYVESANT AND THE WALL

*T*he colonial fire department in New York, with its relentless energy and feats of heroism, might, in earlier times, have accrued a mythical origin—perhaps a priesthood for Prometheus or maybe forty firefighters springing, fully equipped, out of Zeus's head. But in the modern eighteenth century, it was more about politics than mythology. The fire department was a political creation, enabled by an act of the provincial legislature in 1738 and implemented by the aldermen of the town's city council. Moreover, the fire department was not simply an organizational innovation that complemented the technical innovation of the fire engine. It was part of a firefighting culture, over a century old, where every man, woman, teenager, town official, enslaved person, merchant, soldier, sailor, doctor, teacher and preacher was expected to, and consistently did, physically fight fires.

DUTCH ROOTS

The roots of this century-old culture were Dutch. Unlike the English colonies in New England that sought freedom from religious persecution, the Dutch colony on Manhattan was a corporate enterprise, created for profit. Since the 1620s the States General, the Dutch legislature, had granted the West India Company (WIC) a monopoly for "trade opportunities" bordering the Atlantic Ocean, which included Africa, South and North America and the Caribbean.[11]

The Dutch modeled the WIC after the successful Dutch East India Company (the abbreviation in Dutch was VOC).[12] The VOC was established in 1602, and it is often considered the first modern corporation with a broadly based stock offering providing its initial capital. More than a trading company, it built ships, trading posts, forts, had its own navy and army and negotiated treaties with local rulers. It extended Dutch commercial and political influence in India, Indonesia, Japan, Thailand, Vietnam, Taiwan, Malaysia and South Africa.

The VOC had replaced the Portuguese in Africa and Southeast Asia, including Indonesia, by force when persuasion failed. A quasi-military commercial venture, the VOC in the seventeenth century dominated the lucrative spice trade and other high-value commerce, such as textiles, porcelain and silk. The WIC outpost on Manhattan focused its business efforts on bartering with the indigenous peoples, Native tribes and confederacies, whose cultures had flourished throughout the Western Hemisphere for millennia before the arrival of the Europeans.

The principal products of interest to the Dutch were furs, especially beaver pelts, which enjoyed a premium price in Europe for the making of felt for hats. Natives traded for tools, knives, muskets, bullets and gunpowder. In exchange, they delivered up to eighty thousand pelts during a good year in the 1640s and 1650s.[13] The value of a pelt in the Dutch currency of the time fluctuated between 6 and 8 guilders, which resulted in a revenue of about 600,000 guilders in the best years.[14] The table *Exchange Rate of Guiders and Pelts* gives a rough idea of a "consumer price index" for the mid-seventeenth century.

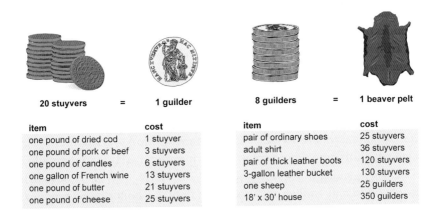

| 20 stuyvers | = | 1 guilder | | 8 guilders | = | 1 beaver pelt |

item	cost		item	cost
one pound of dried cod	1 stuyver		pair of ordinary shoes	25 stuyvers
one pound of pork or beef	3 stuyvers		adult shirt	36 stuyvers
one pound of candles	6 stuyvers		pair of thick leather boots	120 stuyvers
one gallon of French wine	13 stuyvers		3-gallon leather bucket	130 stuyvers
one pound of butter	21 stuyvers		one sheep	25 guilders
one pound of cheese	25 stuyvers		18' x 30' house	350 guilders

Exchange Rate of Guilders and Pelts with Typical Costs for Goods.

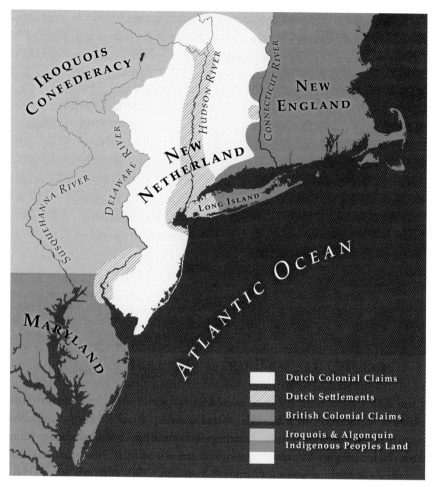

The colony of New Netherland, centered on the Hudson between the Delaware and Connecticut Rivers.

The WIC needed all the revenue it could garner, because as a quasi-military corporation, it had the expenses of a small navy and enough troops to take over Portuguese outposts in Brazil. The Dutch government likely viewed the WIC as its best option to project its commercial and political influence in the Atlantic region, since it maintained the WIC without substantial profit for more than a half century. The WIC colony of New Netherland included the New Amsterdam settlement on Manhattan, villages in western Long Island, large estates and towns along both sides of the Hudson River up to present-day Albany and sites along the Delaware River. There was also a fragile presence along the Connecticut River.

The inhabitants of the colony, reflecting the commercial motivation of the corporation, came to New Netherland for a better economic life. They brought with them a religious tradition of tolerance, rare in the days of Protestant and Catholic orthodoxies. They also brought an organized firefighting tradition, firefighting tools and fire prevention strategies, which included a night watch.

The colonists imported construction tools to build their homes and warehouses. Their principal building material was wood. It came at low cost from the wooden wilderness at the edge of the settlement. The preponderance of a flammable material like wood used for buildings, furniture, wagons, ships and fuel guaranteed the colonists would need to exercise their firefighting culture early and often.

It was more than the usual sparks from wood chimneys or the odd bolt of lightning that underscored the need for effective firefighting in the Dutch colonial period. While they were carving their city out of the wilderness, as though their hard-scrabble life was not grueling enough, the colonists had to contend with potential fires from two sometimes aggressive competitors—Native tribes and the English. Since their essential beaver trade was dependent on good relations with the Native tribes, it is difficult to comprehend how the Dutch would mismanage their way into disastrous conflicts with them, but they did. The raids from both sides often resulted in the burning of the other's settlements. And even before the English Crown decided to annex the Dutch colony, English colonists were probing New Netherland's boundaries along the Connecticut River and on Long Island. These conflicts prompted extraordinary fire prevention strategies, the first of which was a Manhattan-wide wall initiated by the WIC-appointed leader of the colony, Peter Stuyvesant.

Stuyvesant Arrives

Upon his arrival in 1647 as the WIC's director general of New Netherland, Stuyvesant found the colony in turmoil. The previous director, William Kieft, had attempted to impose "contributions" from neighboring Manhattan tribes, ostensibly for Dutch military support against other Native tribes. The tribes ignored the thinly veiled extortion. Kieft then used a flimsy claim of pig poaching on Staten Island to send out a one-hundred-man punitive expedition against the Raritan tribe, killing several, including the Raritan chief's brother.[15]

Kieft's raids provoked a hostile response from the Native tribes. They burned outlying homesteads and killed, captured and drove out farmers and their families. There was a nominal truce in 1643. But then Kieft supported another killing expedition into Connecticut, abetted by English colonial mercenaries. The Native response was a series of devastating raids all over southern New Netherland. The attacks drove settlers from their farms; many were killed before they could escape. Their homes and barns were burned. Many survivors came to Manhattan, where more than one ship carried disillusioned colonists back to the Netherlands. Commerce withered throughout the colony. The valuable fur trade, bottled up as it was in Fort Orange (Albany), ceased. Under Kieft's tenure, Manhattan looked more like a refugee camp than a prospering settlement.[16]

Back in Amsterdam, the West India Company was horrified that its director, in less than five years, had misdirected the colony into virtual annihilation. Petitions from the troubled inhabitants of New Amsterdam and damning reports from their own employees prompted the company to act. As it surveyed its roster of potential directors to replace Kieft, it came upon a candidate who seemed ideal, a skilled administrator with broad experience in the Americas and a dash of military knowledge. He was courageous, indefatigable and, most importantly, a dedicated company man—Peter Stuyvesant.

Stuyvesant was born around 1611 in the northern Netherland state of Friesland. His father was a clergyman, educated at University of Franeker, where Peter also matriculated around 1629. Peter departed Franeker before graduating, probably due to a lack of financial resources.[17] There were scurrilous stories spread by Stuyvesant's political enemies decades after he left Franeker that he was forced to leave for improprieties with his landlord or landlady or landlord's daughter (depending on the story). Perhaps he delayed paying his last month's rent—hardly the scandal as later projected by those who believed with all political sincerity that everything connected with the WIC was fundamentally flawed. Even though he prematurely ended his studies in 1631, he was already well educated; he was literate in Latin and facile in the mathematics used in business. He was skilled enough to get an entry-level job with the West India Company.[18]

Stuyvesant so impressed his employers that after a year, they assigned him to be their commercial agent on the small archipelago of Fernando de Noronha off the coast of Brazil. The Dutch had appropriated Noronha from Portugal and used it as a base to further disenfranchise the Portuguese in Brazil itself. In 1638, he received a promotion to be the commissary of stores, the chief commercial officer in Curaçao, the island center for Dutch operations in the Caribbean. In 1642, on the WIC fast track in his early thirties, he became the director of Curaçao, Aruba and Bonaire.[19]

Stuyvesant's first major opportunity as director came in 1644 with orders to recapture the island of St. Martin, which had been taken by the Spanish a decade before. If he was successful there, it was conceivable that raids might be made into other Spanish Caribbean colonies. In this military enterprise, he would lead three hundred soldiers to storm the Spanish fort on the island. Unfortunately, in the first battle, a cannonball smashed into his lower right leg, which demobilized him and demotivated his troops. After a monthlong fruitless siege, he reluctantly withdrew to Curaçao.[20]

Stuyvesant's leg was amputated just below his knee. As with most surgeries of that type in the seventeenth century, the operation and recuperation were painful, and the wound was slow to heal (two to three months in "ideal" conditions). However, the tropical Caribbean was far from ideal. In its miasmas were a mass of maladies that could infest the wound or infect the patient. Stuyvesant was gravely ill during his recovery, but by the end of 1644, he finally returned to the Netherlands, where he was fitted for his wooden leg.[21]

The West India Company appointed Stuyvesant to replace Kieft as director of New Netherland. He set sail with his family, including his wife, his widowed sister and her four children, finally arriving in Manhattan in 1647. After getting Kieft and his principal adversaries on a ship back to the Netherlands, Stuyvesant settled in to manage the reversal of the colony's misfortunes. He had, at the time, the luxury of peace with the Native tribes, the result of a truce Kieft had managed two years earlier.

Stuyvesant soon discovered, however, that he might have a quarrel with a faction of his own colonists, who had their own ideas of how the colony should be managed. Their agenda was to weaken the governance of the WIC in Manhattan or eliminate it altogether. Since Stuyvesant's mandate was to promote the interests of the WIC, he had an inherent and unavoidable conflict with the anti-WIC faction both in New Amsterdam and the Netherlands.[22]

FIRE ORDINANCES FOR THE TOWN OF WOOD

Still, even with the initial political haggling, most townspeople could appreciate Stuyvesant's leadership in many civic improvements, which crucially included fire prevention. His fire ordinances could not come fast enough for this

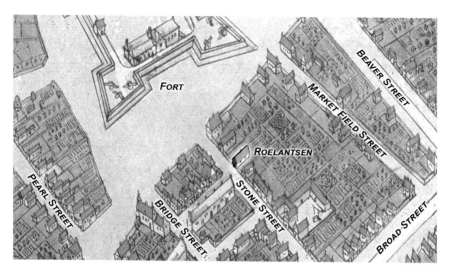

The Roelantsen House, located on Stone Street near the fort.

wooden settlement. Most early Dutch colonial houses used timber frames made with wooden posts and wooden beams, along with wooden rafters and wooden braces connected across bays by wooden joists and wooden purlins and enclosed by wooden clapboard siding.[23] The houses had none of the fire-retardant techniques of modern wood houses, the most noticeable visible difference being the flammable thatch, woven to form a roof.

Typical of the early dwellings was the 1642 house that carpenter Jan Teunissen built under contract for Adam Roelantsen to be located on the north side of Stone Street, near the fort. The house was thirty feet long and eighteen feet wide, with a ceiling that was eight feet high. The roof specified was "a good, thatched roof, properly made," with a tight ceiling of clapboards. Other specifications included three windows, two exterior doors, a vestibule, a pantry, a bedstead, a cased-in stairway to the attic and a chimney with a wooden shaft extending above the roof. The cost was 350 guilders, Holland currency.[24]

Inside, the fires for cooking and heat were never far from something combustible—furniture, clothes and sometimes straw or gunpowder. Stuyvesant had not been in New Amsterdam long before he began issuing ordinances for fire prevention. In January 1648, he published this edict:

> *It has been noticed and seen by the Director General…that some careless people neglect to have their chimneys properly swept.…Lately, fires broke out in two houses and further troubles may be expected…as most of the*

Colonial Dutch House with a thatched roof, clapboard siding, two doors and three windows. An eighteen-by-thirty-foot interior had a front living room and a rear kitchen with a pantry and cupboard bed.

This 1650 wood frame included nine-inch-thick "pi" shaped braces (1), wall plates (2), rafters (3), collar beams (4) and purlins (5). A ladder led to an attic; a side door, to a vestibule hall; and the front door, into the front room.

houses here in New Amsterdam are built of wood and roofed with reeds, also…the chimneys are of wood, which is very dangerous.[25]

He continued: "Henceforth, no wooden or merely plastered chimneys shall be put into any house.…Chimneys already in use may remain…at the discretion of the firemasters." He appointed four firemasters to enforce the ordinance, with the authority to levy and collect fines of three guilders for each instance of a chimney that had not been swept or was otherwise substandard. After deducting the firemaster's commission, the fines were to be used to purchase firefighting equipment, including ladders, hooks and buckets. Perhaps what is somewhat harsh to modern observers was the fine of 25 guilders if anybody's house was burned down from "negligence or his own fire."[26]

The First Anglo-Dutch War

In addition to his ordinances during this period, Stuyvesant also initiated and completed what could be considered a crucial component of his fire prevention strategy, a wall a little over eight feet high across the entire width of Manhattan. The street behind this wall would later be named Wall Street, and it became the financial center for the colony and eventually the country. The wall was to be a defense against a rumored attack from English colonists from New England, coordinated with an invasion force directly from England.

England's parliament had declared war on the Dutch worldwide in 1652. For the English, it was part trade war, part political maneuver. England's civil wars, from 1642 to 1651, pitted the king and his Royalist forces on one side against parliament, led by Oliver Cromwell, on the other. During that decade, England had lost several markets to the Dutch, like those on the Baltic Sea in Germany, Scandinavia, Poland and Russia. Moreover, for Cromwell, it was just as important to eliminate any Royalist influence in the Netherlands as it was to retrieve lost commerce.[27]

Hostilities broke out at sea about one year after the end of the last civil war. In 1653, Stuyvesant received notice from the WIC directors in Holland to shore up his defenses on Manhattan. They believed a destructive attack there by the English was likely.[28] And there was no more effective way to destroy a wooden settlement than to burn it down.

Stuyvesant, along with his provincial and town councils, formed a planning committee to implement a defensive strategy, with several high-priority measures: increase the night watch to full squads concentrated and commanded out of city hall; repair and upgrade Fort Amsterdam's defenses; fully arm a ship to be at ready, day or night, to defend against an invasion by sea; surround the greater part of the city by a stockade to provide those outside the city a refuge and a protective barrier behind which to fight; and devise a plan to raise the funds necessary for these defenses. The financial plan initially called for loans from wealthy colonists, which would then be paid off by a general tax levy over time. The estimated amount necessary for this plan was 4,000 to 6,000 guilders. The initial "contributions" from the wealthy listed in the plan was 5,050 guilders.[29]

The Wall

Within days, the planning committee released a specification for a palisade wall and put it out for bid. The wall was to be 180 Dutch rods long, which was about 662 meters or 2,000 modern English/U.S. feet. The Dutch rods were shorter than English rods (16.5 English/U.S. feet), being 12 English/U.S. feet or 3.68 meters. The Dutch measures for rods, feet and inches are quoted here.

The main component of the proposed wall was a log palisade, "twelve feet long, eighteen inches in circumference, sharpened at the upper end.... At each rod, a post twenty-one inches in circumference is to be set, to which rails, split for this use shall be nailed one foot below the top."[30] The twelve-foot-tall palisades and posts would be sunk into the ground to present a wall nine feet high to the outside. Behind the wall, there was to be a four-foot-tall sod-covered breastwork that allowed sentries to patrol behind the wall.

However, when the bids came in, ranging from 40 to 50 guilders per rod, the committee realized that the wall, as specified, could cost as much as 9,000 guilders, almost double the funds allocated for all the fortifications, including the fort upgrades. Their solution was to redesign the wall. In place of the individual palisades, they would connect the large twenty-one-inch posts with planks fifteen feet long and one foot wide. That meant the nine feet of the wall above ground would have nine planks stacked and nailed into the posts. The committee estimated the project would cost 3,166 guilders, well within the budget.

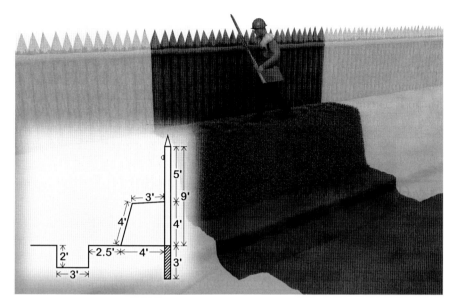

This two-thousand-foot-long defensive wall gave Wall Street its name. It was initially proposed as a palisade of twelve-foot-tall, sharpened logs braced by a packed-earth breastwork that provided a platform for sentries and defenders.

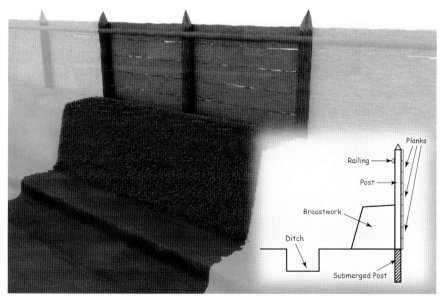

The 1653 plank wall, the first built, replaced the costly all-log design with planks that were fifteen feet foot long and one foot wide connecting thick posts. Later walls (1655–64) may have used the original all-log design.

Replacing the twenty-four palisades of each section with nine planks saved about sixteen guilders per section. The saving in materials for the wall alone was almost three thousand guilders. Moreover, the labor required to nail nine planks to the posts rather than sink each palisade three feet into the ground would be substantially less. The plank wall was finished by mid-March 1653.

With the end of the war with the English in 1654, the urgency to maintain and improve defenses lapsed. According to complaints from the town managers, the wall fell into disrepair, and efforts to extend the wall along the Hudson River stalled.[31] The next year, 1655, however, there was a renewed urgency to improve the defensive barrier. This time, the threat was not from the English but from Native tribes. In the middle of the Native conflict, some would say the cause of it, was the irrepressible provincial secretary, Cornelis van Tienhoven.

TIENHOVEN AND THE PEACH WAR

Tienhoven had been the commander of the one hundred Dutch soldiers sent by Director Kieft on a punitive expedition against the Raritans. He came to the colony as a bookkeeper for the WIC. How the Dutch produced so many presumably mild-mannered administrators, who, without missing a beat, transformed themselves into intrepid warriors to lead military expeditions, was the wonder of the West India Company. Even Stuyvesant himself had no formal military training but still led three hundred soldiers against the Spanish fort on St. Martin. Where did they find these people?

Tienhoven was so patently capable that when Stuyvesant sent Kieft back to Holland, he kept Tienhoven on as the provincial secretary and expanded his role in the management of the colony. In his ongoing disputes with the anti-WIC faction, Stuyvesant also relied on Tienhoven to defuse the faction's machinations in Manhattan against his regime. Stuyvesant even sent him to Holland to defend his policies and governance from the anti-WIC partisans, who had taken their small civil rebellion back to the fatherland.[32]

In Holland, the anti-WIC faction initially prevailed and convinced the States General to order Stuyvesant back to the Netherlands.[33] But the WIC managed to have the order delayed. Then the First Anglo-Dutch War intervened, and the campaign for recall evaporated. Having avoided official censure, Stuyvesant, following WIC directives, initiated reforms for broader political and judicial participation of the colonists, using the model of governance as practiced in Amsterdam. The core of Dutch polity was the "burgher," a citizen who had the right to engage in trade, to form and join guilds, to file suit in court, to participate in town government and to pay taxes. In the 1650s, there were about 250 burghers in New Amsterdam, about the same as the number of households.[34]

In the early 1650s, Stuyvesant would appoint two burgomasters (co-mayors) and five schepen (aldermen) from among the prominent burghers. They comprised the city council that had judicial and administrative duties. They formed the burgomaster-schepen court that tried civil cases, which gradually, over the next decade, increased the scope of their rulings. In addition, they also supervised tradesmen, like coopers and bakers, sometimes in detail (for example: setting the price of a loaf of bread), and administered fire safety reforms and managed the night watch. They were responsible for the financing and construction of public works that could include roads, canals and the defensive "wall" that eventually delineated Wall Street.[35]

Stuyvesant had initiated the wall defense directed at the English threat during the First Anglo-Dutch War. But a long, wooden wall, even in the best of times, needed maintenance. Instead, in the years after the war, it suffered from benign neglect and deteriorated. Then in 1655, renewed conflicts with Native tribes called for an urgent and major upgrade.

Stuyvesant had taken most of the WIC militia on an expedition against intrusive and unauthorized Swedish settlements on the Delaware River. Cornelis van Tienhoven, as the highest-ranking WIC official left in town, was responsible for its defense. Unfortunately, while Stuyvesant was gone, over one thousand warriors, including Hackensacks and Mahicans, came down the Hudson to raid other tribes on Long Island. While they paused at Manhattan for food, a Dutchman shot and killed a Native woman as she plucked peaches from his tree.[36]

The Natives raged into town to look for the offending Dutchman, plundering and burning homes as they went. Tienhoven quickly organized the townsmen and militiamen who were still there. At the time, there was property damage and terrified colonists, but there had been little killing. But when Cornelis ordered the militia to fire on the tribesmen, the Natives responded in kind, and the killing and the devastation of the "Peach War" exploded.[37]

Tienhoven's enemies—and he had quite a few by then—accused him of turning a manageable encounter with the Natives into a bloodbath. Even more, after some mutual killing, the tribes left lower Manhattan and spread into the adjacent countryside, Staten Island and northern Manhattan, where they destroyed settlements, burned farmsteads, killed some settlers and made others hostage. It took Stuyvesant a few months to restore a tense peace. It took him even longer to get most of the hostages returned.[38]

The Wall Reinforced

The Peach War convinced Stuyvesant to reinforce the wall on the northern border of the town. To finance the wall, he imposed a levy based on taxable property on each household. About 6,300 guilders were assessed from 220 taxpayers, which averaged to about 28 guilders per taxpayer or about 3 merchantable beaver pelts. Some inhabitants without cash, or beavers, contributed labor. In the top ranks of the contributors were Director Stuyvesant at 150 guilders and Provincial Secretary Tienhoven, several merchants and shipowners at 100 guilders.[39]

The town reinforced the original wall with planks, each five feet long, that were about the same distance from the top of the breastwork to the top of the interior of the wall. Presumably, they were placed vertically, then nailed into the original horizontal planks. Along with this upgrade to the original wall, Stuyvesant began to extend the wall down the Hudson River. With the added funding, some or all of that wall might have used the original palisade design.[40]

In 1656, the WIC discharged Tienhoven, ostensibly for his part in the Peach War—also perhaps some of his indiscrete letters back to Holland criticizing that the WIC had found its way into the wrong hands. He went missing later in 1656. His hat and cane were found floating in the Hudson River, and his body was never found. He was presumed dead. Stuyvesant, by that time, probably hoped he was. But uncertainty always beclouded his disappearance, because his brother had absconded earlier in the year and later showed up in Barbados. At least Cornelis had the decency to stay gone and never be heard from again.[41]

Fire Ordinances and Fire Buckets

A decade after the first ordinances and two years after the wall was reinforced and extended, Stuyvesant felt the progress in firefighting was too slow. In the fall of 1657, "troubles by fires" prompted Stuyvesant to extend the former ordinances and increase the fines. In previous ordinances, existing wooden chimneys and roofs covered with reeds were exempt from the building ordinance at the discretion of the firemasters. Now the inhabitants had four months to replace the roof covering, rebuild the chimneys and remove haystacks, even those in "chicken houses and hog pens."[42] After four months, any violation would be fined twenty-five guilders. If the house with violations caught on fire, the fine was one hundred guilders, basically a dozen beaver pelts.

Stuyvesant may have been relying on these punitive measures to inspire the general populace into compliance. But only a "great burgher" would have any chance of paying a fine as large as one hundred guilders, and there were only twenty "great burghers" in 1657, less than 10 percent of all households.[43] Perhaps he was depending on the incentive paid to the firemaster to ensure more effective fire prevention. Under the ordinances, they would receive a commission of one-third of all the fines they collected. But no one, not even a burly firemaster, could collect from some poor former homeowner standing among the ruins of his burned-down house, a century and a half before fire insurance and with no pelts in hand.

In any case, by 1657, Stuyvesant was no longer in a mood to wait for fines to fund the purchase of more firefighting equipment. He directed the burgomaster council to levy a tax of eight guilders (or one beaver) on each house. The revenue thus generated was used to buy "100 or 150 leathern fire buckets."[44] If the treasurer collected the eight-guilder tax from all the more than two hundred households (never an easy or certain task), there would be a surplus that was to be applied toward more firefighting equipment, such as hooks, axes and ladders.

As a practical matter, any order for buckets sent to the Netherlands could take the better part of year to be shipped back. To deploy the buckets faster, the burgomasters contracted with two local shoemakers to make 150 three-gallon leather buckets at six to seven guilders each.[45] The order was placed in August 1658. The buckets were delivered and distributed in January 1659— about a third to city hall and a dozen each to nine houses around the town.[46] During this period, individual households often had their own buckets to add to the public supply, and a few decades later, each house was mandated to have two or more buckets. (See the buckets' placements in *1660 Map of Wall* in the "Expanded Wall" section).

Manhattan, under Stuyvesant's direction, developed an approach to fire prevention similar to those of other colonies, like Boston, which included regulations for compulsory chimney inspection, improved building codes and the storage of gunpowder in purpose-built magazines.[47] Their firefighting appliances were three-gallon buckets for the brigades, hooks and axes for the firebreak teams and ladders to fight fires in and on tall buildings. Crucially, every settler had the duty to fight fires in bucket brigades or firebreak teams.

Fire prevention did not stop there. Stuyvesant upgraded and professionalized the night watch with the payments (by 1658, twenty-four stuyvers a night, distributed among the eight watchmen).[48] One of Stuyvesant's highest priorities for the night watch was the early discovery of fires.[49] When detected, the watch would raise the slumbering populace with shouts, bells and loud wooden rattles.

The first responding colonists who were roused by the alarm would sprint to the fire with their own buckets and those thrown into the streets by neighbors not yet fully clothed. Following soon after, others collected the buckets at city hall and the bucket houses. Old engravings show people running from a well to the fire, carrying buckets of water. When enough people were on the scene, bucket brigade lines formed from a major source of water near the fire, such as the rivers, inland canals or wells with cisterns, to the site of the fire. Ideally, the settlers—men and women, burghers and the enslaved—formed a double line, one line passing buckets full of water from the water source to the site of the fire and the other returning the empty buckets from the fire back to the water source.

In larger fires, water thrown on the fire to quench the flames seemed inadequate, and on authorization by town officials, the men with axes and hooks broke up and pulled down houses, sheds and other structures in an attempt to form a firebreak. It was a risky strategy. Whether or not the fire reached the torn down building, its owner would almost certainly seek restitution. If the fire did reach the rubble of a pulled-down house and it had not been doused with water, it would burn faster than an intact house.

By the early 1660s Stuyvesant's New Amsterdam had a population of about 1,500.[50] It was not plagued by as many large fires in the seventeenth century as Boston, perhaps because, with fewer people, it was less-densely

Bucket brigade.

packed.[51] Canal ditches and several wide streets, such as Broadway and Broad Street, while not perfect firebreaks, would at least delay a fire's progress.[52] A long canal down the middle of Broad Street moved with the tides, extending north into the heart of the settlement. And although it would take several decades to get rid of all the wood chimneys, Stuyvesant had managed the settlement to build an increasing proportion of its houses, hearths and chimneys out of brick and stone.[53]

The Expanded Wall

The northern wall across the island, by the mid-1660s, had been substantially expanded and reinforced. The original wall was 180 Dutch rods or a little over 2,100 feet (U.S./English), essentially the width of the island at the city's northern border. Stuyvesant had begun extending the wall down the Hudson River in the late 1650s, and that extension appears on a 1660 map to be about 1,600 feet long. The East River had defensive structures in 1653,

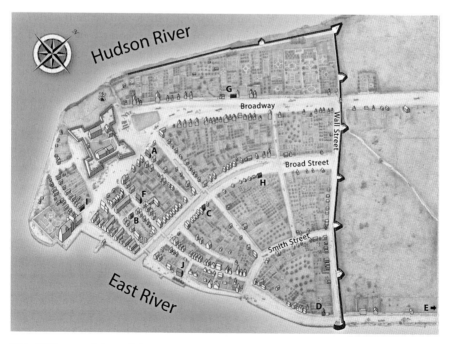

This 1660 map of the wall shows stone bastions with cannons that had been added along Wall Street and an extension of the wall that was added down the Hudson River. The houses highlighted show where the city's fire buckets were stored.

and Stuyvesant may have intended to improve them. But by the 1660s, the Smith Street area was still incompletely fortified.

The major improvements to the northern wall were six bastions of stone projecting out from the wall large enough to accommodate a cannon or two. There was a fortified bastion/gate at the East River and another gate at Broadway and the wall. It is not clear from the illustration whether part of the wall had been upgraded to the palisade design or remained planked. The wall, fully manned and armed and might have been effective, at least in the north, if the attack had been anticipated and if the attackers had only small arms. Against the broadsides from a seventeenth-century warship, however, the walls along the rivers would not last a day.

STUYVESANT'S SECOND MAJOR FIRE PREVENTION STRATEGY

On a bright August morning in 1664, in the plaza outside Fort Amsterdam on the southern tip of Manhattan, children frolicked, pigs snorted and shopkeepers haggled.[54] In contrast to the sweet, peaceful summer morning outside the fort, Dutch troops inside hustled to battle positions. South of the fort, in the mists across the bay, were several warships—English warships.

As Peter Stuyvesant, director general of the Dutch colony of New Netherland, assessed the threatening fleet through a telescope, he saw a squadron of four English warships. He estimated the largest ship to have forty-two cannons; the others had thirty-six, eighteen and fourteen.[55] English diplomats had told Dutch envoys in England that the squadron was sailing to address boundary issues in New England. They had neglected to mention the armament, which was several times more than what a diplomatic mission would require.

Stuyvesant also confirmed that there were troops on the ships, perhaps three or four hundred. Worse, the English militias from Long Island were gathering in Brooklyn across the East River with cavalry and about another one thousand troops. This combined force was coming to Manhattan not to settle a boundary issue but to change one—and not just the boundary but the entire control and possession of the region that had been settled by the Dutch for almost a half century.

Stuyvesant quickly took inventory, first of his troops and gunpowder in the fort and then of the martial spirit of his Dutch settlements. All were meager. Only 150 soldiers in his small garrison were well enough to fight.

Top: Manhattan, August 1664: looking south on Broadway from the wall toward the market at Bowling Green and the Dutch fort defending New Amsterdam.

Bottom: English warships anchored in the harbor beyond the fort came to change the name of the town from New Amsterdam to New York.

Disease debilitated the remaining 50. His supply of gunpowder would not last a day. And the burgomasters, local officials charged with the defense of the towns on Long Island, rejected the notion of armed resistance, even before the British landed their first soldier.[56] To Stuyvesant's request for a draft of every third man, the burgomasters answered, "It is impossible for us to comply…as we ourselves…without protection…[would] leave wives and children seated here in fear and trembling.…Yet we heartily wish it were in our power to assist your Honors."[57]

With Stuyvesant's outer settlements sending their best wishes but no troops and with too few troops of his own, there remained only Stuyvesant's "commonality and subjects" in New Amsterdam itself. Not to be out-angsted by their fellow colonists on Long Island, New Amsterdam's residents sent Stuyvesant a petition signed or marked by ninety-three solid citizens, including Stuyvesant's own son. The distraught petitioners felt "certain" that Stuyvesant would "conclude, with God's help, an honorable and reasonable capitulation."[58]

Stuyvesant decided to stall for time. Perhaps he could organize a defense of the town if he had a few days. But realistically, he knew that unless a Dutch fleet of comparable force sailed into Manhattan's harbor very soon, his capability to resist the British was nil. He sent his lieutenant to ask the British commander about the "purpose" of his visit. Since Britain and the Netherlands were not at war and Stuyvesant had no official notice from Holland, his lieutenant would no doubt affect "surprise" at the visit. Surely this force did not intend to violate the peace.

But that is exactly what Colonel Robert Nicolls, the commander of the English squadron, did intend. He was going to take over Manhattan— by force if necessary—without regard to previous peace treaties with the Dutch. The reigning English monarch, King Charles II, had commissioned Nicolls to sail to America, seize New Amsterdam and the Dutch settlements on Long Island and north along the Hudson, "reducing that people to an entire submission and obedience to…our government, now vested…in our Brother the Duke of York." Charles wanted to perfect English claims to the North American seaboard from Virginia to Maine. He also wanted to "assume" the Dutch trade centered on Manhattan, "which they have wrongfully possessed themselves of."[59]

Apparently, from King Charles's point of pretense, without sanction from an English king a half-century before, the Dutch did not have a legitimate "royal" authorization to settle a colony in North America. To fulfil the king's invention, Nicolls had about one hundred cannons on his four ships and three companies of veteran troops he had brought with him from England. In addition, several colonial English militias from Long Island, previously enjoined from direct military action, then saw an opportunity for some modest looting of Dutch warehouses. If Stuyvesant resisted Nicolls, he would inevitably lose. There would be nothing between the Long Islanders and the valuable stores of beaver pelts, tobacco and wampum, the fungible beads that were used like coins in this colonial realm.[60]

Thus, in August 1664, Stuyvesant faced his most crucial fire prevention decision ever. If he resisted the English invasion, the city would first be shelled with fifty-gun broadsides for a few hours. Then, after the fort and much of the town was rubble, the English colonial militias would come in and set fire to anything they could not steal.

Stuyvesant soon embraced the pacific mood of his minions. He provided the house on his farm for the negotiations that resulted in the Articles of Capitulation. Then, two days later, without firing a shot, Stuyvesant surrendered the fort, marching out in high ceremony with the two hundred soldiers under his command. Thus, in the late summer of 1664, New Amsterdam became New York, in honor of the province's new proprietor, the king's brother and Nicolls's patron, James, the Duke of York.

Charles II's aggressive "trade policy," which, in addition to the takeover of New Amsterdam, included raids on Dutch trading posts along the coast of West Africa and a blatant attack on a Dutch merchant fleet in the Mediterranean, and soon led to war, the Second Anglo-Dutch War (1665). The Dutch, with a new modern battle fleet, financial structures that could keep a large fleet at sea longer than the English and a successful daring raid up the Medway, forced Charles to abandon the war and agree to the Treaty of Breda (1667). The treaty left New York in English hands, but for the Dutch, it secured other "more profitable" territories, such as Surinam in South America, the Banda Spice Islands in the East Indies and the fort at Cormantine on the coast of West African.[61]

Stuyvesant returned to the Netherlands to defend his decision to capitulate. He exchanged heated charges and countercharges with his managers at the WIC. But Stuyvesant had two advantages in the debate: he could decisively document his requests to the WIC for powder and other military supplies, which were ignored, and the Dutch legislature, the States General, which would adjudicate the dispute, had already witnessed the WIC's ineptitude in New York and elsewhere. With the Treaty of Breda, the English kept New York, the assignment of blame became irrelevant and the dispute "died in committee." Stuyvesant returned to New York to live out the last years of his life peaceably on his farm, the Bouwery.[62] He died in 1672, the year that the Third Anglo-Dutch War began.

The debate over Stuyvesant's directorship began within its first eighteen months and waxed and waned for almost twenty years, but it lost most of its steam upon his retirement. However, the director could make a convincing case for his contributions to firefighting and fire prevention. When he arrived, they were primitive and inadequate, but by the time he retired, many components, such as the paid night watch, were a model for British colonies in America.[63]

Stuyvesant's implementation of the Dutch "burgher" system of government efficiently extended his fire safety reforms. The town council appointed fire wardens to inspect chimneys and managed the "rattle watch," the night sentries whose shouts and rattles would alarm slumbering citizens into action to fight a fire.[64] Thus, Stuyvesant's basic system of building codes, building and chimney inspection, firefighting appliances, firefighting techniques, community involvement, the use of the night watch with alarms and fire prevention were the essential ingredients to a system that worked as well as those anywhere else in America and more effectively than most. It would remain fundamentally unchanged until its addition of fire engines in the eighteenth century.

2
THE FIRES OF TWO WARS,
A REVOLUTION AND A REBELLION

*I*f Rip Van Winkle went to sleep in Manhattan after a deep draught of Dutch beer in 1665 and napped for thirty years, he would awaken to a Manhattan with some significant differences. Although the English flag still flew over the fort, the king sharing the throne of England was a Dutchman. There were 4,500 people in New York, about three times as many as there had been before the long nap.[65] More of this expanding population was beginning to live outside the wall, especially along the East River. And by this time, the French and their Native allies had become the principal incendiary threat to both the province and the city of New York.

Our Rip had slept through the Dutch regaining Manhattan and then giving it back to the English after another war. He had also missed the Glorious Revolution in England that replaced James II with his daughter Mary and her Dutch husband, William III. He may have noticed two factions in the town at each other's political throats, which was an improvement over several actual hangings during a short rebellion a few years before.[66] He had also slept through almost all of King William's War, which saw the French and their allies ransack and burn Schenectady. It would no doubt surprise him that 20 percent of the people then in the town were enslaved Africans or their recent descendants. The English were in charge, but the most common language was still Dutch.

TRANSITIONS: DUTCH TO ENGLISH, ENGLISH TO DUTCH AND DUTCH TO ENGLISH AGAIN

After the capitulation agreement, Colonel Nicolls wisely continued the Dutch burgomaster system for almost a year before transforming it to the English system with a mayor and aldermen.[67] Even so, with less than 10 percent of the city being English, the Dutch still participated in virtually every phase of administration, providing most of the first aldermen and virtually monopolizing the firefighting system.[68] The men of the rattle watch, for example, were mostly Dutch and took their orders from Dutchmen in Dutch.[69] Even a generation later, the fire wardens would have names like Peter Adolf, Derck van der Brinke, Derck ten Eyck and Tobeyas Stoutenburgh.[70]

The English system installed by Nicolls lasted for seven years before the English and the Dutch were again at war (the Third Anglo-Dutch War). This time, Charles had finally persuaded King Louis XIV of France to join him to crush the Dutch—Louis by land and Charles by sea. In response, the Dutch sent two naval squadrons independently to raid and exploit English and French possessions in America. Their raids serendipitously crossed paths near Barbados and then combined to attack several Caribbean islands and relieve Virginia of its tobacco crop. They also recaptured Manhattan after a violent cannonade of two thousand rounds. After accepting the English surrender, the Dutch commanders reinstituted Dutch civil governance in 1673, and the burgomasters were back in business.[71]

Meanwhile, the Dutch needed to get the English out of the war quickly so they could focus on the French, who had already invaded the southern Dutch provinces. Yet another incentive for a fast settlement, if one were needed, was the fact that Spain would not join the Dutch against France until the English quit the war. Fortunately, Charles was in a mood to bargain. The war with the Dutch was unpopular, particularly among the influential merchant class that had lost several hundred cargo ships to Dutch privateers.[72] For Charles, the war was ruinously expensive, and the awful violence of the large Anglo-Dutch naval battles resulted in no advantage, strategically or financially.

The Dutch guided the Treaty of Westminster toward status quo ante, in which each side retained what they had before the war. It was simpler and had a better chance for rapid resolution than the sluggish yearlong, negotiated-for-profit Treaty of Breda (1667), in which each side retained what they had taken during the war. The English—that is, James, the Duke of York—got Manhattan back with the Westminster Treaty in 1674.[73]

Although New York was caught in the middle of the Anglo-Dutch wars of the seventeenth century, its three "management" changes from 1664 to 1674, from Dutch to English, English to Dutch and finally Dutch back to English, did not impede the development of its firefighting. The only large-scale violence that took place in the three transitions came from the Dutch ship cannons when they retook Manhattan in 1673.[74] And far from radicalizing the new citizens of New York with an alien hegemony, many Dutch considered Nicolls and his successors to be at least as congenial as Stuyvesant. They continued their support of the community-based firefighting with bucket brigades and hook-and-ladder teams with enthusiasm.

From 1674 to the end of the seventeenth century, despite the political turmoil in England and the consequent political schism in New York, the city's firefighting system more than survived, it expanded and became more effective. It depended, as before, on the fire wardens, the night rattle watch and bucket brigades. And it was winning the battle against wooden chimneys and thatched roofs. A 1676 report to the common council by Constable Robert Whitte stated: "Persons that have noe Chimnyes [*sic*] or not fit to keep fire in: Claus Ditlos…Adam Miller…Cobus de Looper… Isack Molyne." The dozen or so householders in Whitte's list were ordered to build or repair their chimneys within three months or be evicted.[75] This severe penalty, now narrowly applied to just a dozen households, suggests that the former "shilling" fines that were broadly applied were no longer needed. Since the 1660s, chimneys had increasingly been made of stone or brick. The shingle roofs that replaced those made of thatch below the wall of Wall Street were less of a fire hazard.[76]

WARDS

A few years later, in 1683, James II sent a new provincial governor, Thomas Dongan, to New York with a broad directive to improve the governance and financial return of the province. Dongan, a longtime Royalist supporter of James, fully embraced his mandate and soon collaborated with New York colonists to write new charters for both the province and the city. These charters confirmed, expanded and further delineated the "rights, priviledges [*sic*] &c" as conveyed by Nicolls. The city of New York's self-governing corporation and charter, official in 1686, although operating de facto from 1684, was unusual in colonial America. Boston did not

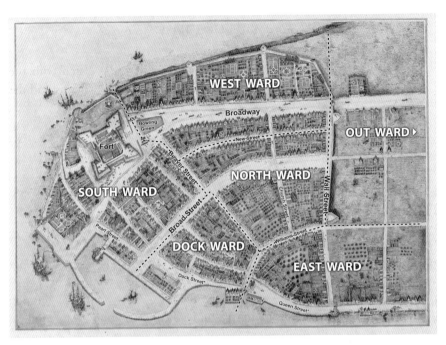

This 1700 map of wards shows six wards, the basis for the city's administration, each of which had two fire wardens to enforce fire codes. By then, the wall in the East Ward had been removed.

receive a city charter for another century and a half.[77] The charter also updated fire prevention policies by incorporating them into the town's new "ward" system.

The Dongan Charter organized the city into six wards: East, West, North, South and Dock were at the southern tip of Manhattan, "inside the wall" of Wall Street, and the Out Ward, which encompassed all of Manhattan north, or "outside of the wall."[78] Each ward elected an alderman and assistant alderman. The mayor and a recorder, appointed by the governor, joined with the aldermen and assistants to form the city's common council, which was responsible for the city's legislation and administration.[79] Also chosen for each ward were assessors and a constable, whose responsibilities, in addition to the general mandate to secure law and order, included providing "a list of the names of all male persons… sixteen years old and upwards" to the mayor, who would choose from it the all-important night watch.[80]

NIGHT WATCH AND BRICK

The night watch had become known as the Constable's Watch with the English return to power in 1674 and would draw on both civilians and the militia for ample coverage. However, Dongan explicitly exempted the militia from the watch soon after his arrival. Later, when a governor thought that an invasion was imminent—as was the case in 1689, when the French and their Native allies ransacked Schenectady at the beginning of King William's War (1689–97)—the responsibility for the watch quickly and entirely devolved to the militia. When peace was restored, the watch reverted to civilian control, reporting directly to the mayor. By the turn of the century, the watch was referred to as the "Bellman's Watch," denoting the bell the watch would ring periodically and then "proclaime [*sic*] the season of the weather and the hour of the night."[81]

Other ordinances of 1684 prohibited "hay, straw, or other combustible matter within their dwelling houses" and a fine of fifteen shillings "if any person suffer his chimny [*sic*] to be on fire."[82] In 1686, every house with two chimneys was required to provide a bucket that was to be taken immediately to the fire by the householder or, if they were unable to respond, thrown into the street for others who were sprinting to the fire to pick up. Other bucket quotas included: houses with more than two hearths, two buckets; brewers, six buckets; bakers, three—with a penalty of six shillings for every bucket left "wanting."[83]

In addition to empowering the common council to manage inspections and issue fire ordinances, the Dongan Charter enhanced fire prevention in subtler ways. The charter bequeathed all vacant land on Manhattan to the city corporation. The common council no doubt viewed this land as a valuable, not-easily-renewable asset, and as such, it was in no hurry to sell it. However, the corporation needed income to pay for the Dongan Charter—the "rights, liberties, priviledges [*sic*], advantages, emoluments &c" were not free.[84] They also had in mind other projects, such as a new ferry house and a new market house, which needed to be funded.[85] So, the council began selling "water" lots along the East River, creating Dock Street and then Queen Street. Significantly, the houses on Queen Street were required to "be two full storyes [*sic*] high above the ground and the front to the street to be either brick or stone."[86]

The use of brick and stone for building, at first fashionable and then specified as a condition for purchase of municipally owned lots, turned New York into a city less apt to burn.[87] It did not experience the large-scale fires during the seventeenth century that Boston, for example, did in 1679. The newer buildings, especially below Wall Street and along the East River, were built by wealthy merchants with an eye to the style and substance of the colored bricks favored in Dutch design.

In 1697, a visitor from Boston, Dr. Bullivant, remarked that "most of their new buildings are magnificent enough" and made with "Flanders" brick.[88] Sarah Kemble Knight, also from Boston, noted in her diary from a 1704 visit that the buildings were generally made of brick of several colors and "laid in Checkers, being glazed, look very agreeable." She also noted another Dutch-inspired fire deterrent: the extensive use of tiles in and around fireplaces and also on "the walls of the kitchen, which had a brick floor."[89]

Boston visitors admired New York's brick and stone buildings and perhaps believed that they would prevent a major fire like Boston's in 1679. In that twelve-hour conflagration, seventy warehouses, eighty houses and several ships were destroyed.[90] But brick and stone were never the principal building materials used in colonial New York. The principal material was wood. Often, the "brick house" had only a façade and fireplace made of brick and stone. The rest of the building was made of wood. As Richard Howe observed in *Material City*, "neither brick nor stone—both of them fireproof—could even begin to match the winning combination of wood's availability, cost, tensile and compressive strength, workability, and durability."[91] But as he also noted, "Wood burns, and so do wooden cities." Boston, as a wooden city, demonstrated that proposition in 1679. It would take New York almost a century to show that it, too, was a wooden city and that it, too, could burn.

In summary, from 1674 to 1700, New York's population rose from 3,000 to about 4,500, with most living in the lower five wards.[92] The 809 households consisted of 5 to 6 people on average. However, since some houses contained more than one family, the average number of people per house was closer to 7.

The city continuously improved the fire safety of its buildings, enhanced its firefighting capability and intensified its fire inspection. In the 1670s, when the canal down the center of Broad Street was filled in, several wells were dug to replace the canal water for firefighting.[93] By 1696, the city's sixteen wells were put under the supervision of the alderman and assistant alderman in each ward so "that they be kept sweet usefull [*sic*] and in good repair."[94]

At the end of the English war with the French in 1697, the northern wall began to be disassembled, as housing in the East Ward expanded north. The aldermen and assistants were also tasked with appointing and managing the

Population

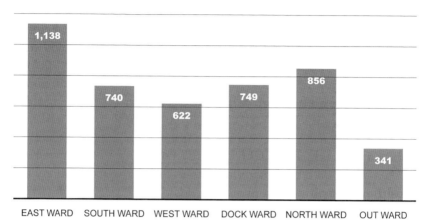

The 1703 New York census showed the city was home to 4,446 people in 809 households in its six wards.

chimney inspectors, two for each ward, who were to make weekly inspections of every chimney and hearth in their area.[95] Thus, in the last quarter of the seventeenth century, New York firefighting was capable and organized, surviving and thriving in the political turmoil of several regime transitions, two transatlantic wars, a few tribal conflicts, a remote revolution and a short rebellion. There were no devastating domestic fires, little arson and New York's incendiary enemies were kept at a safe distance.

3

UPRISINGS, ENGINES AND THE CREATION OF THE FDNY

New York's Slave Revolt

The census of 1703 put the population of New York at 4,446, but the census was more than just a headcount. It delineated sex, age and race.[96] Considering the demographics of other northern colonial towns, perhaps the most distinct feature of this census is the proportion of the New York's population that was enslaved. Enslaved Africans and their descendants comprised almost 20 percent of the city's population. Moreover, since freed people and their households were not included in the census, there is little doubt that they were undercounted in 1703.

Slavery was imbedded in New York as it was nowhere else in the American colonies at that time. Over 40 percent of households had enslaved people, two to three on average for those households. Not surprisingly, wealthier households tended to have more enslaved people than households of modest means.[97] New York's distribution of the enslaved among so many households differed from the concentrations of the enslaved on plantations that already existed in the West Indies and were emerging in the southern colonies. Slavery in New York was more widespread and a greater part of usual household life than anywhere else in America.[98]

Unfortunately, New York's variation of involuntary servitude, perhaps not as oppressive as that in the West Indies, was still mean and cruel and became meaner and crueler in the eighteenth century. At least under the Dutch regime, the enslaved could be manumitted and then participate in New Netherland's commerce, more or less, as other settlers. The New York regulations, modeled after harsh English practices in the Caribbean, prohibited freed people from owning land or a house. Even that restriction was eclipsed in the early 1700s, when it became financially punitive for a master to free an enslaved person in the first place.[99] There were also restrictions on the enslaved walking at night, gathering in groups larger than three and buying or selling anything. Whippings, beatings, shackling and other harsh physical punishments were allowed by law and applied as often as the White masters felt necessary.[100]

In 1712, New York had its first slave revolt. It caused the deaths of three dozen people. In reaction, as if there had been some loopholes in the earlier laws, the common council passed seven pages of laws proscribing and restricting what the enslaved could do, when and how they could do it and whom they could do it with.[101] There would have been more onerous laws had the governor, Robert Hunter, and his council not revised the original proposals from the city—at least that is what Hunter reported to the Lords of Trade in London.[102]

According to Hunter, a little after midnight on April 6, 1712, "about three and twenty" enslaved people got together in an orchard in the center of town and armed themselves with muskets, swords, knives and hatchets. Hunter believed that the enslaved were intent on revenge for "hard usage…received from their masters." They set fire to a shed and waited for the first White people to respond, and when they arrived, they began to shoot, stab and axe them. Nine White people were killed, and six were wounded.

Those who escaped the first ambush spread the alarm, and Hunter himself ordered a detachment of soldiers from the fort to put down the rebellion. The rebel enslaved withdrew to the woods. Hunter posted sentries on Manhattan's exits so that the rebels could not escape and then ordered militias from the city and county to "drive the island…[making] strict searches in town." Scores of enslaved people were arrested; six killed themselves before they were captured.

Of those who went on trial, almost all were found guilty. Twenty-one were executed—"some were burnt, others hanged, one broke on the wheele [*sic*], and one hung alive in chains in the town, so that there has been the most exemplary punishment inflicted that could possibly be thought of."[103] Five of those who were tried were acquitted by the court or otherwise reprieved by Hunter.

Later, during the Maroon Wars in the 1730s, Hunter was the governor of Jamaica. He died there before the former enslaved people broadened their freedom and autonomous rule over several regions of the island. As educated and experienced as he was, Hunter must have been troubled that he could not resolve a way to pacify thousands of enslaved who organized, armed themselves and began a real rebellion. New Yorkers who had lived through the first slave revolt must have had similar unsettling thoughts. They had experienced the inherent risks of the brutal oppression and ruthless coercion of so many people.

The pervasive possibility of rebellion, from small personal paybacks to larger reprisals, inspired fear and deep-seated anxiety in American slave owners and their families.[104] New York was no exception. As a fretful article in the *New-York Gazette* put it: "I would have each and every one of us...not to forget the great Calamity...in the City of New-York some years since, by the Negros rising there and murdering many good innocent people, and if it had not been for His Majesty's garrison there, that city [in all likelihood] had been reduced to ashes and a greatest part of the of the inhabitants murdered."[105] The article referred to the recent uprising on St. John's and the successful revolt on Jamaica to explain "the general melancholy apprehensions of His Majesty's subjects in the West Indies." The article suggested "some great fatality attends the English dominion in America, from the too great number of that unchristian and barbarous people being imported, and then by some too much indulged in their vices."[106]

As disturbing as the New York slave revolt may have been, it did not affect the basic racial demographics of the city over the next two decades. The natural growth of the enslaved population from births to enslaved couples and the continued importation of enslaved maintained their proportion of the population in the city. The census in 1712 showed 5,841 people lived in the city, and about 17 percent of them were enslaved. The census of 1731 counted 8,622 people, with a little over 18 percent of them enslaved.[107] Over this period, about 30 percent of the enslaved population were children. In the households of 1703, about 70 percent of the households with enslaved people had enslaved adults and children, providing the possibility at least of a Black family within the household.[108]

The ethnic mix of the White population did shift. The city was becoming more English. The proportion of residents of British ancestry increased from about one-third in the early 1700s to almost one-half in 1730, while the ethnic Dutch population decreased from about 50 percent to 40 percent over the same period. In 1731, the French contingent made up about 9 percent of the city's population, while identifiable segments of Portuguese Jews and Germans in about the same proportion

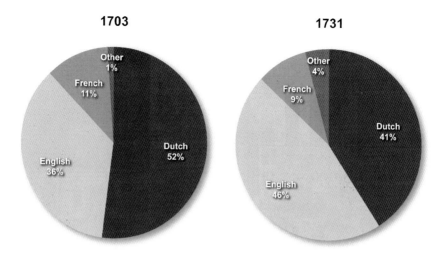

Dutch to English ethnic shift in New York between 1703 and 1731.

comprised the remaining 4 percent of the White population.[109] New York was more heterogeneous than other British colonies in North America— multiracial, multiethnic, and multidenominational.[110]

THE NEWSHAM ENGINE

Slave revolts often included the destruction of property, and a very thorough way to destroy property was to set it on fire.[111] Every instance of an enslaved person retaliating against their master may not have been publicized, but no fire was too remote or too small for the newspapers of the time to report. There were routine accounts in New York's papers of one of London's disastrous fires. In 1731, the *New-York Gazette* reported on page 2 that a fire in Wedel, Germany, had destroyed the entire market town near Hamburg, except for the church and five houses.[112] But an entire town did not have to burn to reach page 2 of the *Gazette*.

In 1734, a fire in a wigwam in Narragansett Rhode Island also made page 2. Its brief article told of two unfortunate children who had died while their parents were "from the house."[113] The *Gazette* reported on fires of natural, intentional and accidental causes from all over the world.[114] Closer to home, detailed stories of Boston's large fires and Philadelphia's small fires projected the dire possibilities for New York.

Inspired by revolts, fires, reports of fires and the spirit of their new Montgomerie charter with its emphasis on fire safety, New York's common council finally, in 1731, commissioned Stephan DeLancey and John Moore to purchase two Newsham fire engines in London and transport them to New York.[115] By 1725, the date of his second patent, Richard Newsham had refined and combined several technologies to produce man-powered engines that could throw large volumes of water, one hundred gallons per minute, forty yards or more.[116]

The common council had enough information to specify an engine of the sixth type and an engine of the fourth type with auxiliary equipment— "suctions, leathern pipes and caps (nozzles)." They might have gotten details from contacts in Philadelphia (who had recently ordered engines) or Boston (who had been ordering engines for fifty years because the town burned down so often). They may have even corresponded directly with London, where engine makers were building and promoting the machines.

The council authorized the purchase of sixth and fourth type engines. The city's agents purchased newer models of Newsham's engines (designated as fifth type and the second type) that had comparable performances and lower prices.[117] Apparently, the city benefited from a fire engine competition in London between Newsham and a Mr. Fowke of Nightingale Lane in East London.

Newsham's 1725 broadside promotional sheet listed his best £60 engine as having a discharge rate of 170 gallons per minute. Fowke eventually countered with a £60 engine that was capable of streaming 180 gallons per minute, 10 gallons more than Newsham's. Moreover, Fowke's lower-priced engines also offered better a discharge and projected the stream to greater distances than the comparable Newsham. Newsham had some catching up to do, either in actual development or in advertised claims.

According to a contemporary survey, by the time New York had purchased its first engines, Newsham had upgraded his entire line of engines.[118] His newest fifth type engine held in its cistern (water tank) a few more gallons than his previous sixth type. While its discharge rate was a little lower, it had an improved range and cost less. This upgrade was why, no doubt, New York's agents bought a new fifth type and eschewed the old sixth type. His new second type had range comparable to his old fourth type.[119]

Any engine specified to discharge over 120 gallons per minute would stream the equivalent of at least forty leather buckets a minute, so it was quite a challenge for the bucket brigades to keep the engine's cistern filled.

Richard Newſham, *of* **Cloth-Fair, London,** *Engineer*

Number of Sizes.	What Quantity of Water the Cifterns hold in Gallons.	Quantity dif-charg'd per Minute in Gallons.	At what Number of Yards Diftance.	Price without Suction.	Price with Suction.
1 ft.	30	30	26	18 *l.*	20 *l.*
2 d.	36	36	28	20	23
3 d.	65	65	33	30	35
4 th.	90	90	36	35	40
5 th.	120	120	40	45	50
6 th.	170	170	40	60	70

A London broadside, circa 1730, promoting Newsham's fire engines.

Anticipating that difficulty, Newsham designed a hand-operated valve that could switch quickly—in a second or two without affecting the stream—from the "internal" supply, the engine's own cistern, to an "external" supply, which came through a hose, using the engine's suction to draw water from a river or well reservoir.[120]

Another clever feature, not invented by Newsham but applied to substantial advantage in his man-powered machines, were the mechanical linkages from the long handrails on the sides of his engines to the pistons of the pump. Previous machines had "direct-lever" connections from the handrails to the pistons, which tended to employ longer lever arms to get more force to the piston and a greater velocity of water through the nozzle. However, longer lever arms also meant a more cumbersome engine, which was often heavier and too wide to get through London's narrow passages. Newsham's solution to this problem was to insert a "wheel-and-chains" linkage that acted as a gear between the side handrails and the pistons. The force on the handrail was thus "leveraged" by the gear to increase the force on the piston and the velocity of the stream. This allowed Newsham to use

This 1725 Newsham fire engine had a one-hundred-gallon water basin (1), housing for the pump (2), a swivel nozzle (3), two pull-down handles (4), foot treadles (5) and wooden wheels (6) that supported an eight-foot-long frame.

"close-hauled" handrails and resulted in a more compact machine. Even his largest engines could get through passages about three feet wide.

As was previously mentioned, Newsham did not invent the "wheel-and-chains" gearing mechanism. It was described and illustrated in an earlier patent.[121] However, Newsham did incorporate an elegant implementation of the "wheel and chains" gears along with a unique treadle system that could separately, or in conjunction with the handrails, power the pistons. Men would stand on the engine, steady themselves with a pair of fixed rails attached to the frame of the engine and shift their weight from foot to foot, like a modern stepping exercise machine, on two treadles that worked the shafts of the pistons. The primary benefit of the treadle system was that more men could simultaneously work the pump. A secondary benefit was that the machine could work in a narrow space powered only by the treadles on the engine. Newsham's design did not require space for extra men pumping the rails of the engine.

The originality of the Newsham engine was not in any specific innovation. Rather, it was in Newsham's systematic application of a multitude of "state-of-the-art" components to the engineering of his machines, their design and

These x-ray engine views show handles/treadles connected to bow-tie gears and chains. The rear gear drove two pistons inside their cylinders, forcing water into a continuous-flow compressor.

construction. For example, one refinement that was developed in Germany and Holland in the seventeenth century had the piston push water into an air vessel and then used the compressed air pressure inside the vessel to drive a constant stream of water out through the nozzle—a large improvement on the intermittent spurts that came from a piston when used alone. His engines used an air vessel in conjunction with a two-piston pump.[122]

The larger of the two engines New York purchased was the fifth type. It had a cistern that could hold 176 gallons and was specified to discharge 160 gallons per minute to a distance of fifty-eight yards. With the quick-switch suction feature and six feet of suction pipe, the price was £50. The streams of water from this large Newsham engine could reach the highest part of all but a few buildings in New York at the time.[123] This was a vast improvement over a bucket brigade that could not reach a top floor or roof unless they entered a burning building or used ladders that leaned on the building itself—both dangerous practices. The common council authorized £200 (equivalent to $40,000 in the twenty-first century) for the purchase and delivery of the machines and auxiliary equipment to New York.[124]

The machines proved to be well worth the investment, even though it is unlikely New York's engines performed "as advertised" in Newsham's confident literature. The first and weakest link was not in the engines but in getting water to the engines. The hoses, incidental items of the purchase, were not widely used anywhere in colonial America, certainly not in New York. That meant the cisterns of the engines had to be filled by a bucket brigade. If a bucket were delivered every three seconds (and it would have to be a very coordinated brigade to do that), the stream would be limited to sixty gallons per minute, less than the maximum flow specified for even the smaller engines.

On the other hand, Newsham's claim of a 160.0-gallon outflow per minute was probably exaggerated. The volume of each fifth type engine piston was about 0.6 gallons, which means that if both pistons were emptied every second, the outflow would be closer to 70.0 gallons per minute rather than 160.0. At half that pumping rate—still a vigorous exercise—the outflow would be 35.0 gallons per minute. If a bucket brigade could manage to fill the cistern at 30.0 to 60.0 gallons per minute and if the pumping crew could pump a full cycle every second or two (35.0 to 70.0 gallons per minute), the input would more or less match the output. Newsham's modest overestimate would not make a substantive difference. It would only matter if the engines were hose-fed, which did not happen in America until the nineteenth century.

TURK AND THE FOUNDING OF FDNY

The Newsham engines were shipped from London in September 1731 and cleared New York's custom house in the last week of November.[125] The timing could not have been better, as they were cleaned, oiled and ready for action when, around midnight on a Monday, a few days later, "a fire broke out in a joiner's house in this city. It began in the garret, where the people were all asleep, and burnt violently; but by the aid of two fire engines…the fire was extinguished, after having burnt down the house and damaged the next."[126] At the time, there was no fire department. In fact, there was no one individual in charge of maintaining the engines. The town magistrates (mayor, aldermen, constables) managed the engines and directed the firefighting.[127]

This loosely managed firefighting equipment must have seemed adequate—perhaps because there were no fires in New York noteworthy enough for a mention in the newspapers. However, the common council, in early 1733, did appoint an "overseer," Anthony Lamb, to maintain the engines, which were then housed in city hall.[128] He was "to put the fire engines in good order, and also…to look after and take care of the same, that they may be always [sic] in good plight and condition & fitt [sic] for present use."[129] In addition to ensuring the engines were always in proper working order, Lamb also directed the first response efforts of the townspeople. Lamb, as the first "overseer" of the engines, was paid a salary of twelve pounds a year, plus expenses.[130]

A few months into Lamb's tenure as overseer, he responded to a fire that broke out in a cooper's shop on Smith Street and burned down the shop and an adjoining stable before being contained by streams from the engines and extinguished.[131] Later that year, the engines were instrumental in saving the house of Gerardus Comfort and a ship that was being built nearby on the banks of the Hudson River. The fire started when a crack in an oven that was baking bread spread to Comfort's workshop and stable, both of which burned down. The fire "burnt with great violence by reason of a high wind."[132] But with the fast response of the inhabitants and fire engines, the fire "was extinguished, without doing any other considerable damage."[133]

Throughout the first years of their deployment, the engines continued to prove their merit, quenching small fires quickly and containing large fires before they were out of control. In 1735, Henry Ryer's house was burned in a furious fire, but once again, the timely arrival of the engines saved the houses next door.[134] In early 1736, the corner house next to the Meal Market caught fire, but the flames were extinguished quickly.[135]

Later that year, the city council moved the engines, which were then housed in city hall, to a building that was specially designed for the engines and other firefighting tools.[136] It was built next to the watch house in the middle of Broad Street, close to Wall Street.[137] The common council also appointed Jacobus Turk, a gunsmith with broad mechanical experience, to be overseer, a post he held for the next twenty-five years. Turk not only maintained the engines from England but also experimented with the development of a small fire engine, the first in New York to be financed by the city itself. Perhaps the generosity of the city paying for his engine development persuaded Turk to take only ten pounds a year for being overseer.[138]

In the winter following his appointment, Turk faced his first big test. A large fire broke out on a Sunday afternoon in John Rosevelt's stable. It destroyed the stable and two manufacturing buildings and damaged a linseed oil mill and three houses. The quick and sustained response from the fire engines and colonists brought the fire under control in two hours.[139] However, the *Gazette* reported that magistrates suspected several enslaved people and brought them in for questioning. The paper's editor felt the mere possibility of the enslaved being culpable vindicated the restrictions of the town's onerous slave ordinances.[140]

Although enforcing restrictive ordinances may have made some people feel good, several influential leaders felt that they did not translate into putting out fires more quickly. For that, they believed the city needed trained firefighters. Within a year after the large fire, these leaders began to work in the provincial assembly and common council to substantially enhance the city's firefighting capability. Their plan was to organize and mobilize a dedicated corps of specially trained firefighters, colonial Gotham's FDNY.

In 1738, with authorization from the provincial assembly, the common council established what was, in effect, the city's first fire department "a sufficient number of strong, able, discreet, honest, and sober men" to maintain, manage and use the engines and other fire tools "which persons… shall be called the firemen of the City of New York." For their city of eleven thousand people, the provincial assembly had specified forty-two firemen as the maximum "sufficient number." The common council appointed thirty men to establish the department, five from each of the six wards "south of the fresh water," including the new Montgomerie Ward.[141]

The creation of "firemen," with their unique obligations, duties and privileges, was, in many ways, as much of an innovation for New York as its municipal charter. Every adult New Yorker had the duty to fight fires, but they were seldom fined if they showed up late or not at all. Certainly, no one expected them to muster into groups just to practice fighting fires. On the other hand, the new firemen were to be fined if they did not quickly deploy to an actual fire or attend the monthly practice and maintenance sessions. In return, although they were not paid, they were exempt from jury duty, the night watch, serving as a constable or in any other unpaid civic post. And, as important to many of them over the next four decades, they were exempt from the monthly routine of militia duty. Of course, if the city was in danger of attack, and they were expected to muster as an armed militia quickly.

New York's first volunteer firefighters were middle-class, skilled tradesmen with moderate assets, as demonstrated by the occupations of the first thirty: five carpenters; four blacksmiths; four coopers; four cordwainers; three bakers; two each of block-makers, brickmakers, carmen and gunsmiths; and a sutler and a ropemaker. (Cordwainers made shoes, not to be confused with cobblers, who just repaired them. Sutlers sold provisions to the military.) Among those first appointed in 1738, one of the gunsmiths was Jacobus Stoutenburgh.[142]

Jacobus was the grandson of Pieter Stoutenburgh, an early Dutch colonist, who, during his five decades in Manhattan, contributed to the colony's civic life in a host of roles that included arbitrating land disputes, curating the estates of orphaned children and serving as the town treasurer. He and his wife, Aefje, had nine children, five of whom reached adulthood. The last to be born was Isaac Stoutenburgh, Jacobus's father.[143] Jacobus was born in 1710. His father, Isaac, unfortunately died at the age of forty-three the year after Jacobus was born. After his father's untimely death, his mother, Neeltje, raised Jacobus (who was one year old at the time of his father's death), along with his older siblings Maria (eight) and Isaac (six), probably with the help of her eldest son, Peter, who was nineteen.[144]

By the time Jacobus was in his teens, his older brother Isaac was old enough to have completed his "internship" and begun working as a gunsmith. It was likely that Isaac influenced Jacobus to become a gunsmith also. Another influence was probably Jacobus Turk, ten years his senior, whose sister Maritje Turk the young Stoutenburgh married when they were in their early twenties. In addition to their professional and familial relationship, both Turk and Stoutenburgh had an interest in firefighting that was heightened by the arrival of the first fire engines. In fact, drawings of the engines from this early period have been attributed to the then-twenty-one-year-old Jacobus Stoutenburgh.[145]

Turk himself had become the "overseer" of the engines the year before the colonial legislature authorized the fire department of which Stoutenburgh was a charter member. In addition to developing fire engines as mentioned previously, Turk has also been credited with many firefighting innovations, not the least of which was the design of the leather fire helmet that was worn by New York firemen for over a century.[146]

Turk directed the firefighting of his firemen and the colonists whose rapid response was still relied on to form bucket brigades. While the mayor and aldermen had, in principle, the highest authority in the management of firefighting, it was Turk's job to be there first with his trained crews and the equipment, engines, ladders, ropes, hooks and extra buckets, all of which he was commissioned to maintain in good condition. He would direct the engines and then coordinate the first bucket brigades.

As with Lamb, Turk would leave the decision for firebreaks to the city magistrates. Nobody wanted his or her house or business torn down, even if it seemed to be in the best interest of containing a fire. One could imagine a business owner yelling to his alderman in the din of a large fire, "Take Bayard's warehouse down; he has four others…leave mine alone!" Dismantling buildings to form a firebreak was always contentious and could result in lawsuits.

In the 1730s, New York was fortunate to have only one or two newsworthy fires a year. However, over the decade, there seemed to be about as many reports of enslaved people's revenge, plots or rebellions as there were serious fires. One rebellion on the island of in St. Kits resulted in a half-dozen houses being burned. In a conspiracy closer to home in Eastern New Jersey, enslaved

Mid-eighteenth-century firefighting included a Newsham-type fire engine filled from a well by a bucket brigade and pumped by hand by a half dozen firemen. Others brought hooks, ladders and salvage bags.

people plotted to burn houses and barns but were betrayed by a comrade and arrested before any fires were set.[147] Also in Amboy, New Jersey, Phillip Kearny's enslaved teenage boy "set his master's barn and stacks of corn and hay on fire, and destroy'd [*sic*] it all."[148] So, although the new and improved fire department and its engines had reduced the chance of fires getting out of control, the stories in the papers kept the fear of slave uprisings in New York's collective conscious.

Part Two

DEVELOPING THE "MODERN" COLONIAL FDNY (1740–75)

The Newsham Engine—the first engine used by the FDNY before the Revolution.

4

THE "REVOLT" OF 1741

THE FDNY'S FIRST BIG TEST

*T*he fires began on March 18, in the governor's house inside the century-old fort, then called Fort George, at the southern tip of Manhattan. With the first alarm, townspeople could see large volumes of smoke emanating from the center of the roof. At first, no flames were visible. Soon, however, from the east section of the roof closest to the chapel, the flames broke through. Then, almost simultaneously, more flames leaped out in several places across the roof.

A strong wind drove the fire to the chapel next to the governor's house as the Newsham engines were on the ground but working to less-than-full effect in the turbulent air. Even though the fire raged out of control at the governor's house, the engines were redirected to the secretary's office outside the fort walls but next to the governor's house in the hope of saving the colony records. These efforts delayed the advance of the flames enough to allow almost all the official documents to be rescued. However, the fire inside the office, as it did in the governor's house and chapel, "burned with a fury, that no human power could extinguish it."[149]

As the firefighters battled the fire at the barracks and other buildings inside the fort, there was a rumor spreading faster than the flames that gunpowder stored inside the fort was in danger of exploding. Ready to fight fire but not explosions of gunpowder, many men abandoned the fort, even though George Clarke, the lieutenant governor, assured the firefighters that there was no powder stored there. Clarke's information was only partially accurate. Although there may not have been any kegs of powder stored in the fort, there were some hand grenades. When the grenades began to explode, those who were still fighting the fire inside the fort got out fast.

Even so, it was likely by then that most of the buildings in the fort were lost. "In about an hour and a quarter's time, the house was burnt down to the ground, and the chapel and other buildings beyond human power of saving."[150] The last line of defense was at the stables outside, between the fort and houses next to the Hudson River. As the stables began to burn, a few embers reached the shingles on the roofs of the houses. A providential rain and the continuing efforts of the townspeople stopped the fire at the stables. A special watch was assigned to guard against a flare-up from the last timbers that still burned and then glowed until morning.

No one at the time thought the fire was deliberately set. Lieutenant Governor Clarke supposed a plumber accidently started the fire while he was repairing a gutter between the house and the chapel.[151] The plumber carried with him, as tools of his trade, a soldering iron heated by coals in a firepot. Perhaps the coals launched a spark onto the roof of the house to burn there unnoticed. But careful observers noted that a fire from a spark on the roof would burn from the outside in, rather than the reverse—what witnesses saw was smoke on the roof coming from a fire on the inside, without any flames on the roof at first. Still, "no one imagined the fire was set."[152]

On March 25, a week later, there was another fire. At the southwest end of town, the old, shingled roof of Captain Warren's house was ablaze. The Newsham engines were on the scene early, played with good effect and put out the fire. A large section of the roof was gone, but the house itself did not suffer much damage. Some attributed a faulty chimney to be the cause of the fire, which was a reasonable enough possibility.

On April 1, a week after Warren's fire, there was yet another fire, this time near the East River at the Van Zant storehouse, an old wooden building, which contained ultra-flammable pine boards and hay. The fire was already in the roof when it was discovered. With its flammable inventory and the many wood buildings next to the warehouse, many despaired for the neighborhood. Luckily, the storehouse was near a slip, a slightly larger-than-boat-sized inlet where boats could dock, secured from the flow of the river. Buckets were easily and quickly filled from the slip and conveyed to the Newsham engines.

At the same time, to reduce the potential fuel for the fire and to abate its ferocity, some men actually entered the building, removed the pine boards,

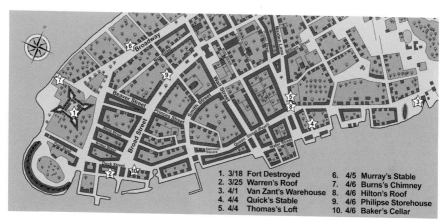

1. 3/18	Fort Destroyed	6. 4/5	Murray's Stable
2. 3/25	Warren's Roof	7. 4/6	Burns's Chimney
3. 4/1	Van Zant's Warehouse	8. 4/6	Hilton's Roof
4. 4/4	Quick's Stable	9. 4/6	Philipse Storehouse
5. 4/4	Thomas's Loft	10. 4/6	Baker's Cellar

Fires in 1741, ten in succession over three weeks, destroyed the fort and a warehouse and damaged eight other buildings. Hysteria from the arson resulted in the execution or deportation of over one hundred enslaved people.

some of which were beginning to burn, and threw them into the slip. The Newshams and the firefighting spirit of many New Yorkers stopped the fire. The warehouse was completely destroyed, but almost miraculously, the neighborhood was saved. Someone's best guess as to the cause of the fire was that a man was smoking his pipe too close to the hay. But the fire was seen on the roof before the hay caught fire. More than one colonist believed the fires had been set. The town with two or three large fires per year had just experienced several major fires in less than a month.

Three fires on April 4 and 5 convinced the city's residents. These fires were not accidental but caused by arson. The first alarm went up from the old district called the Fly, near Quick's house. A pile of hay was on fire in the middle of a cow stable. With early detection, it was easily quenched. Early detection also saved the house of Ben Thomas (next door to the west from Captain Sarly) from a fire in a loft above his kitchen.

Apparently, the fire was set between two beds placed together, one of which was made of straw. No one knew who started the fire, but it was noted that an enslaved person slept in the loft. The next day, coals were discovered under a haystack near the stables of Joseph Murray. The coals had apparently been lit and singed the hay but went out before igniting it. A trail of coals and ashes were tracked back to a nearby house, "which caused a suspicion of the negro that lived there."

FOUR FIRES OF APRIL 6

The fires continued on Monday, April 6. The first fire was a chimney fire in the house of Sergeant Burns, opposite the Fort Garden. But Burns testified that the chimney had been swept only three days before, which should have prevented any chimney fire, let alone one that produced smothering smoke throughout the whole house. In their fear and high anxiety, the people of New York were no longer looking for reasonable possibilities—they were looking for villains. Perhaps the villains were stealing household goods and furniture while householders were out fighting fires. One thing seemed certain: there were too many fires in too many places to be the work of one villain. There were several arsonists, perhaps working in concert.

The next fire broke out two hours later. It was on the shingle roof of Mrs. Hilton's house. It was discovered early and put out, leaving just a little damage to the shingles. Upon investigation, it was apparent that an arsonist had set the fire by placing a burning bundle of flammable fibers on the wall timbers supporting the roof next to the shingles that caught fire. To many, it seemed more than a coincidence that this fire had taken place on the east side of Captain Sarly's house, just two doors down from Ben Thomas's fire that had occurred less than twenty-four hours before. Soon, "there was a cry among the people, the Spanish negroes…take up the Spanish negroes."[153]

An English privateer who lived in New York, John Lush, had captured a Spanish ship and brought it back as a prize in 1740 with nineteen Black and mixed-race sailors. Rather than being treated as prisoners of war, they had been condemned to slavery and sold as part of the prize. The sailors had protested their enslavement, claiming they were free men under their king. But, the admiralty court, with little or no sentimental consideration for a Spanish king, especially during the ongoing war with Spain (1739–48), rejected their arguments, as it had for virtually all captured, Spanish Black and mulatto sailors.[154] At their auction, Captain Sarly purchased one of the Spanish sailors. Then the two houses of Sarly's next door neighbors had been set on fire. The paranoid populace did not have to look far to find their probable culprits. One was in the neighborhood. They arrested Sarly's Spaniard and then went to arrest "all the rest of that cargo, in order for their safe custody and examination."[155]

The third fire on April 6 broke out later in the afternoon, while the Spaniards were still being questioned. A "streak" of fire ran from the bottom to the top of the wood shingle roof of Colonel Philipse's warehouse. The engines, which were housed not far from the warehouse, were on the scene quickly, and almost as quickly, the fire was out. If the engines had not proved their value before, they did that day, especially at Philipse's. It was one of three warehouses—the center building—and was made of old, combustible timber and even more flammable wood shingles. The buildings themselves were enough fuel for a conflagration. With no fireplaces in the warehouses, the nearest sparks from fires would had to have come from houses separated by large gardens from the buildings. Thus, a considerable distance insulated the warehouse from all domestic sparks. Clearly, the fire was not accidental. It was set.

The fourth cry of fire on April 6 came as the warehouse fire was almost extinguished. Because it was under control, most people there sprinted toward the sound of the new alarm. Near Coentes Market, the cellar of a baker was smothered in smoke. A pile of wood chips had ignited there, burning brightly enough to be seen through the smoke—but not fast enough to be out of control. With virtually every bucket in the city then mobilized, the fire was rapidly extinguished. This particular fire may have been an accident, but it did not matter much. By then, the whole town was freaked out.

While the last fire of the day was being attended near the market, back at Philipse's warehouse, Jacobus Stoutenburgh, while climbing around the upper stories of the building to ensure no embers would reignite, saw an enslaved person leap out of a window and run through the gardens, so called out, "A negro; a negro!" And that was soon expanded into an alarm "that the negros are rising."[156]

Some firemen who recognized the enslaved person, Cuff Philipse, were at a loss to explain an alarm more suitable for an armed rebellion than the flight of a single fugitive—who was probably just returning to the Philipse house. However, most people were beside themselves with the horrific spectacle of the day's dangerous fires. A crowd converged on the Philipse house, dragged Cuff out, lifted him completely off the ground, above their shoulders, and carried him to jail. Unfortunately, the hysteria continued. A general dragnet through the streets pulled in "negroes…many had been assisting at the fire…who were met in the streets, after the alarm of their rising, were hurried off to jail."[157]

By the weekend, virtually all of those who had been pulled in on the mass arrests were discharged. That left the city brooding over the fires of the previous three weeks: the destruction of the governor's house, the chapel, the barracks and other buildings in the fort along with the secretary's house; the burning of Van Zant's and Philipse's warehouses; the close calls the at the houses of Warren, Thomas and Hilton; the seemingly "accidental" fires at Burns's and the bakery; and the early detection of two potentially dangerous fires at Quick's and Murray's stables, both of which were clearly caused by arsonists. Daniel Horsmanden, a justice on the New York Supreme Court who was, by then, leading the investigation into the wave of fires, concluded that the fires were purposely set "by some villainous confederacy of latent enemies amongst us."[158]

The city's response was to offer rewards to anyone who revealed the arsonists or their conspirators on the condition that the felons were convicted. A White person would receive a reward of £100 (equivalent to $20,000 in the twenty-first century). An enslaved person who came forward with a "discovery" (identification) of the arsonists would be freed, paid £20 and pardoned, even if they were implicated in the plot. The master of any such enslaved person would receive £25. "A free negro, mulatto, or Indian, to receive forty-five pounds, and also be pardoned, if concerned therein."[159]

The rewards were a reasonable enough initiative at this stage of the investigation. Horsmanden certainly supported them. However, an extension of this system would have an unintended consequence that Horsmanden never fully appreciated. In the case where the enslaved person was arrested and accused, they could still be pardoned if they became a convincing witness and accused others, especially if they had not been accused before. After being arrested, the reward and manumission were off the table, but being pardoned was better than being tried and hanged. The enslaved talked among themselves and knew what Horsmanden wanted to hear, so when they were arrested and interrogated, they told him. They might even embellish the "accepted" conspiracy theory by implicating someone they had a grudge against. Some "confessions" would later implicate White people as well as enslaved people. Horsmanden was soon to get more "latent enemies" than he had dreamed of in his "villainous confederacy."

HORSMANDEN'S THREE BIASES

However, in formulating and perfecting his conspiracy theory, Horsmanden exercised several unfortunate biases. The first bias was to believe, wholeheartedly and uncritically, at first, the testimony of Mary Burton, a White teenage servant who was indentured to a tavern owner. Another bias was that the enslaved, by themselves, were incapable of organizing and executing a conspiracy of the magnitude and complexity as the one he was uncovering. He believed they needed a White leader. Perhaps if he had known more about the revolt of 1712, he might not have been so adamant in this particular bias. But when Mary Burton "reluctantly" testified in her first day before the grand jury that her master John Hughson had repeatedly plotted with dozens of enslaved people to burn down the town and kill White people, it reinforced his predisposition. Horsmanden had his White coconspirator.

While Hughson provided Horsmanden with his White conspirator, he was not a very satisfactory leader of so massive and intricate a plot. Horsmanden wanted a more sophisticated terrorist, one who was literate and trained to inflict mayhem. Thus, to develop his conspiracy theory, Horsmanden exercised his third bias: a vitriolic hatred of Roman Catholicism, especially its priests. For him, priests were tools of the international Catholic conspiracy that was directed by the pope from Rome and supported by England's traditional Catholic enemies, France and Spain. To perfect his theory, Horsmanden needed a Catholic priest, a Jesuit would be a plus. As it happened, while he failed to identify a real Catholic priest, Horsmanden was able to manufacture one, the unfortunate John Ury.

Ury tutored and preached and had some unorthodox theological views, but he was not a Roman Catholic. He needed a good lawyer but could not afford one, and none were otherwise forthcoming. Horsmanden, on the other hand, could rely on a half-dozen of New York's finest legal minds who were working for the king.[160] He was also privy to testimony that he could reveal or suppress depending on how well it fit his conspiracy theory.

Mary Burton had sworn in her first deposition: "That she never saw any White person in company when they talked of burning the town but her master, her mistress and Peggy."[161] When she accused Ury and other White people, she perjured herself. In Ury's case, Horsmanden ignored the perjury. Later, however, when Burton began to accuse prominent White people in the city, he suppressed both the names and the accusations. Although she was allowed to perjure herself when it was convenient for Horsmanden, he later admitted that Mary Burton, when giving a "fanciful" testimony against upper-class White people, was an unreliable witness.[162] To Horsmanden, she became unreliable at the exact moment her testimony no longer fit his theory. In fact, she was unreliable long before that.[163]

By the time of Ury's trial, which included the two enslaved people who were hanged for stealing before they could be convicted and burned for the conspiracy, twenty-nine enslaved people and three White people had been executed—thirty-two in all. Ury, although not Catholic, was found guilty and hanged. He was not the only person convicted without a fair trial.[164] The jury returned a guilty verdict in every single case. How many were innocent? There were ten fires, each likely attributed to one or two people. Perhaps fifteen people were culpable arsonists.

That left Horsmanden's tenuous conspiracy to explain why almost one hundred other people were killed or deported. He did the best he could in his journal, which was published in 1744 and included detailed narratives of the investigations and testimony at the original trials. His exhaustive defense of his decision to hang and deport so many people does not seem very convincing today. It was an ugly excess, even by the standards of colonial slavery.

Aftermath of the 1741 Fires

For the inhabitants of the city, the fires in 1741 were traumatic. Perhaps they were not as large as other colonial fires in Boston and Charleston, but they were disastrous enough. The fort complex was destroyed, homes and businesses burned, families fragmented and hundreds of people arrested, dozens executed and scores deported.

The epidemic of fires could have been worse. At least no one was killed in the fires. Moreover, the outbreak in New York came after the deployment of trained firemen with fire engines. If not for the firemen and engines, several of the fires that were quenched during the "revolt" would have spread to other buildings, burning neighborhoods, rather than just one roof or warehouse. Effective firefighting still took energetic participation by the general populace, but the firefighters' ability to direct large flows of water at potential flash points had been the crucial factor in limiting the damage and saving lives. As the trials of the "conspirators" began, the city ordered another large engine from London and ninety new buckets.[165]

The addition of the engine was only the beginning of the city's response to the "revolt" fires. Over the next year, it would appoint more firemen, build and equip firehouses, drill wells for a better water supply, buy a larger signal bell and fund an expanded the night watch. There were also the inevitable additions to the slave codes. In addition, although perhaps not part of the organized response, there was a dramatic reduction in the proportion of male to female enslaved people, which reversed the growing trend of the enslaved population from the previous decade.[166]

The common council's agents in London were able to negotiate for the authorized investment of one hundred pounds sterling and the purchase of a large engine and one of medium size also. In preparation for doubling their number of engines, the council nominated and appointed fourteen additional firemen, two or three from each of the six southern wards. These firemen were tradesmen, much like the original thirty had been, with three cordwainers, three carpenters and another gunsmith among them.[167] The council also authorized three aldermen, including Isaac Stoutenburgh, Jacobus's brother, to manage the construction of an engine house for the new engines. The same aldermen were enjoined to hang a new, larger bell to supplement the old bell, which was rehung. These bells were rung to alert the citizens of fire and other emergencies.[168]

The Night Watch

Perhaps the real measure of how radically the 1741 fires disturbed the city's leaders came at the end of the year, when they quadrupled the number of people who participated in the night watch. Consequently, since the night watch was, by culture and custom, a paid service, the city raised a special tax to cover the increase in cost. The funding for the first year of the new and improved watch was about £570, more than the council had spent cumulatively in the previous five years.[169]

However, the council's funding for this enlarged watch did not come from ordinary revenues, like the funding for the previous watches. It was made possible by a special tax approved by the state assembly to fund the plan for one year. What would happen the following year, eighteen months after the trauma of the "revolt" fires, if there was no special tax?

The council restructured the watch once again. Gone were the highly paid managers and even the paid watchmen. In their places were constables and unpaid volunteers. In response to the "revolt," there was an expanded mission specified in this law "for apprehending negros and other slaves and for preventing the conspiracy and insurrection of them within this city."[170] The first overseer of the night watch, appointed in September 1743, was Isaac Stoutenburgh.[171]

Isaac Stoutenburgh was born in 1705. Unlike his brother, Jacobus, who was five years younger, he could remember his father, also named Isaac, who died when young Isaac was six. Isaac's mother, Neeltje, raised Isaac, Jacobus and a daughter, Maria, in the family's modest house in the North Ward.[172] Isaac was apprenticed as a gunsmith and felt sufficiently established to woo and wed Anneke Dally in 1733. With Anneke, he had three daughters, two of whom lived into the nineteenth century. His son, also named Isaac, would become a well-known patriot and soldier in the American Revolution.

Isaac Sr. himself had become prominent enough in the community by 1740 to be elected to the city council.[173] During his first six months as a councilman, the fires of 1741 erupted. As part of the institutional response to the fires, Isaac was on the council committee to manage the construction of the engine houses for the new engines being shipped from London. While on the common council, he was also appointed as the overseer of the night watch to manage the cumbersome "volunteer" system that had just been introduced. Isaac remained the overseer for almost three decades during both the volunteer systems and later, when the watch returned to be a professional, paid organization. In fact, it would not be an exaggeration to characterize New York's prerevolution watch as the "Stoutenburgh" night watch.

5

WEALTH FROM THE WARS

THE FDNY EXPANDS

THE TURK YEARS

Jacobus Turk, as overseer, managed the fire department from its inception in 1738, through the rampant arsons of 1741 and for the next two decades. He developed the department as the city council increased its membership to forty-two firefighters and four engines by 1742—it was an efficient and effective firefighting force. In fact, his direction of the engines and his intrepid firefighters stopped many fires that were thought to be unstoppable at first discovery.

On a freezing January night in 1747, a cabin boy on the ship *William* neglected to fully extinguish his candle as he retired. Around 9:00 p.m., the fire onboard was visible from shore, "which, at first view, seem'd [*sic*] to have a terrible prospect…began to blaze out furiously." The *William* was frozen between two other ships in ice that could not support the weight of a man. It looked like all three ships would be destroyed along with their cargoes; the *William* itself was loaded with rum and flaxseed. The crews also were in grave danger. The firemen, however, "notwithstanding the great difficulty and danger, at length got an engine to play upon her and so happily extinguished it."[174]

Although the newspaper report does not describe how they were able to do it, the firemen must have rushed one of the smaller engines into a boat. Then the fire team must have broken through the thin ice and pulled the oars of the boat with enough force to ice break the bow through the harbor to get close to the *William*. Thirty yards from the ship, they could begin to vigorously pump the engine, which streamed water, thirty gallons per minute, directly on the vessel.[175] These firemen were a special breed. They mustered out on a bitter-cold night in January, rowed into the middle of a frozen harbor and pumped a fire engine to put out the flames of a blazing ship most had given up on. This was the FDNY from its inception: selfless, energetic, skilled and highly motivated.

There was no doubt that the firemen were capable of rapidly deploying their engines over water. In April the next year, a fire broke out in a building next to the city's ferry on the opposite side of the East River in Brooklyn. It took some time to get the engine across the river, even though the river and the wind were calm. The New York firemen quenched the blaze—but not before it had consumed the ferry house and an adjoining barn that belonged to the city.[176] The limit to the damage at almost any large fire was determined by how fast an engine and water could be on the fireground.

In April 1749, a terrible fire broke out in Duke Street, where houses were tightly packed. It was not discovered until the roof of the house where the fire started was entirely in flames. "But by good providence, the wind being low, the diligence and activity of our inhabitants soon got the mastery of it, though with great damage to several houses adjoining, and the entire destruction of that wherein it broke out; pieces of burning shingles were carried by the flames to great distance, and several other houses thereby much endangered."[177]

In the same edition of the newspaper that carried the story of this fire, there was an article that suggested several improvements to the city's fire prevention strategies. Having recently observed the problem with flammable shingles, the author proposed more fire-resistant materials for all roofs, either slate or tiles. The city ignored this suggestion for a few decades. The author also proposed to increase the number of engines so that there would be at least one in every ward. Apparently, this suggestion, coincident with the large fire on Duke Street, struck a more resonant chord with the town's leaders, because within a month, the common council ordered two more engines.[178]

This fire of 1749 demonstrated—and the article also called out—that as valuable as the FDNY, with its firemen and engines, was, there was always the third indispensable component to firefighting: the motivated and energetic people of New York. In bucket brigades, they brought water to the engines. Sometimes, they would help form a firebreak or would provide access to the flames inside a building by using the department's tools or their own.

More than once, they fearlessly attacked a dangerous blaze to the awe and gratitude of their fellow townspeople.

In 1745, lightning struck the new Dutch Church, igniting a fire high in the cupola. The fire was discovered and, through the exertions of a carpenter, Francis Davison, and a couple of others who climbed up to the cupola "at the hazard of their lives, and of having the lead melted about their ears," an opening was axed in the exterior of the cupola, allowing water to reach the fire and extinguish it.[179] The church rewarded Davison and others with its deep gratitude and twenty pounds.

A couple of years later, on a cold morning in January, the roof of city hall was ablaze. Once again, Davison climbed to the rescue, "(being the same person that was so instrumental in extinguishing the fire formerly in the cupola of the new Dutch Church) who got out upon the roof with an axe, and cut the roof open where the fire was, the engines at the same time playing the water upon him" and through the opening on the fire itself.[180] The fire was soon quenched. The day had been so cold that Davison himself was "cloathed [*sic*] with ice." The city rewarded Davison with seven pounds (two other men received four pounds) and the high honor of the "Freedom of the Corporation," which was usually bequeathed to war heroes. What motivated Francis—his duty as he saw it, the honor of his fellow citizens or the possibility of a reward? Or was he just trying to impress Elizabeth Jeanelin, whom he married the very next year?[181] Everyone loves a hero.

In New York, between wars (1748–55), discussions on firefighting improvements focused on fire engines and the delivery of water. Among the suggestions, usually made in newspapers or magazines and often addressed explicitly to the common council, were the addition of fire engines, both small and large. One article noted that the smallest engines were priced low enough (fifteen to twenty pounds) that several hundred individuals, albeit prosperous individuals, could easily afford to purchase and deploy one or more engines on their properties for use in their neighborhoods.

The common council endorsed the idea of more buckets and engines. In 1758, they ordered four more engines "one large fire engine, one small ditto, two hand ditto" from London. After the arrival of the engines the next year, they were distributed so that each lower ward had at least one engine—some had two. The common council could afford to be generous with the engines and buckets, because then, during the Seven Years' War (1756–63), the New York economy was booming.

WEALTH FROM THE WAR

In fact, from 1740 to the early 1760s, the colony of New York was the economic beneficiary of British wars with France. To support the twenty-five thousand soldiers and fourteen thousand mariners in America, the British primed the colonial economies as it never had before.[182] In June 1756, Benjamin Franklin, then in New York, witnessed the one thousand troops of two regiments (Thirty-Fifth and Forty-Second) disembarking from six ships of the Royal Navy and the sumptuous dinners given the officers: "oxen, sheep, fowls, strawberries, cherries, pease, &c."[183] "This only I can plainly see, that New York is growing immensely rich, by money brought into it from all quarters for the pay and subsistence of the troops."[184]

Also adding to the wealth from war in New York were the privateers, old warships or merchant ships refitted with armament to enable them to capture enemy "prizes," that is, ships with cargoes. Sanctioned and commissioned by the government, privateers captured prizes worth millions of pounds during the mid-seventeenth-century wars. New York privateers alone "redirected" £2 million into the coffers of its investors, which, not surprisingly, were usually its wealthy merchants.[185] Becoming the largest privateer enterprise of any North American port, the scale of the New York operation was impressive. On any given day during the Seven Years' War in New York, there could be twenty to thirty privateers refitting and reprovisioning to sail.

For example, on June 27, 1756, the *New York Gazette* listed twenty-three privateers in the harbor, with an average of about twenty-eight guns and one hundred men each.[186] This was about one-third of the total privateer fleet sailing out of New York. The other two-thirds of the fleet on this fine June day cruised the Atlantic and the Caribbean Oceans, capturing and plundering French merchant/privateer ships—or even a Dutch merchant ship if it looked like it was carrying French goods.

However, some ships returned without any booty; others did not return at all. There was always a chance of running into a French naval ship or, more likely, a better-armed French privateer. An American schooner sailing from Africa to St. Kitts was taken by enemy privateers three times in the same day. The first took all the cargo, plus those who were enslaved in Africa and on their way to the Caribbean, provisions and the ship's mate, perhaps for his knowledge of other merchant targets. The last two privateers did not even bother to take over the ship, as they did not want to waste any valuable booty time on a cargo-less vessel.[187]

While most of the wealthy were getting wealthier, the rank and file benefited, too. The thousands of sailors on the New York privateers would receive their share of the prizes, most of which was recycled into the New York economy. In addition, those who enlisted directly with the provincial militia or regular support services could receive a fifteen-pound bonus, which was what the New York legislature felt was necessary to compete with Connecticut and New Jersey offers, not to mention privateers. It was such a bonus that enabled the New York legislature, reimbursed by the British government, to enlist almost three thousand recruits in 1758.[188]

THE PROFESSIONAL NIGHT WATCH

During the Seven Years' War (1756–63), New Yorkers were enriched as they never had been before. They amassed their substantial wealth by supplying the king's army and navy, privateering for fun and profit, and smuggling provisions to the French in Canada and the Caribbean. Toward the end of the war, it must have occurred to the beneficiaries of this new wealth that neither their property nor their persons were well protected by an amateur watch. The climate of residents' opinions, as expressed by one irate citizen, was that a watch properly staffed and managed would at least be able to prevent "the many burglaries, street robberies, &c. happening in this city." He disparaged the amateur watch as more than simply inadequate: "The city watch…is a parcel of idle, drunken, vigilante snorers who never quelled any tumult in their lives…but would, perhaps, be as ready to join in a burglary, as any thief in Christendom."[189]

By 1761, there were apparently enough drunken snorers on the watch to move the provincial assembly to action. The assembly passed a law authorizing the city to raise taxes, £1,800 the first year, to fund a professional watch and improve the city's lighting.[190] The common council formed a committee for the task. In February 1762, it advertised in the newspaper and soon had a full complement of watchmen.[191] The council also increased the number of public lanterns. An expanded force of lamplighters maintained and lit the oil lamps nightly. With improved lighting and twenty or more professional watchmen on duty each night and during some days, the city was soon better served and more adequately protected.[192]

The dramatic increase in the watch/lamp budgets would not have surprised Isaac Stoutenburgh, as intimate as he was with the inner workings of the city. For twenty years, he had woven himself into its infrastructure. A typical payment in 1757 itemizes his many roles:

> *Ordered…the treasurer of this city to pay to Mr. Isaac Stoutenburgh—thirteen pounds…for cleaning and repairing the city hall—four pounds… for smiths work done to the poor house—twenty-one pounds…for the constables days & nights watches—one pound, ten shillings…paid to Matthew Wool for a half year's lighting the city lamps—three pounds for advance money for lamp oil…audited and allowed of by this board.*[193]

Isaac was a one-man Department of Public Works.

From 1761 to 1769, the city's annual payments managed by Stoutenburgh for the watch and city lighting escalated by an order of magnitude—from about £100 to about £2,000. These payments reflected the city's new emphasis on domestic security. More importantly, unlike the city's reaction to the 1741 fires, this larger budget was more than a one-year spike. It was a long-term commitment funded by the substantial wealth in the city by those who saw it in their best interest to maintain law and order. It continued from 1762 until the discontinuity of the Revolution in 1776.

Funding

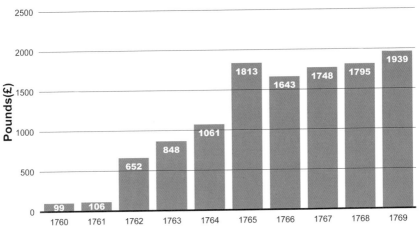

Funding for the Night Watch and city lights was made possible by the wealth gained from the war with France.

As always, a vital task of the watch was to detect fires. If they could not control and quench them quickly, they would rattle, ring and roust the firemen and populace to rapid response. The sooner the discovery and alarm were made, the faster the firemen could have machines on the fireground with people bucketing water to them. Since the deployment of engines in the 1730s, the firemen and the people demonstrated, time and again, that if they got to the fire quickly, they could save buildings, sometimes blocks of buildings—not to mention barns, breweries, mills and ships.

THE STOUTENBURGH FDNY (1761–75)

In 1761, there was also a notable change in the fire department. Jacobus Turk, who had been the overseer for the last twenty-five years, retired and was replaced by Jacobus Stoutenburgh, his brother-in law and a twenty-three-year fire veteran. Turk's department, by 1761, consisted of forty-two firefighters, seven from each lower ward. The machines he had received, repaired and maintained included four large engines, four medium/small wheeled engines and two smaller hand-carried engines. With ten engines distributed throughout the city in several fully equipped engine houses, New York was no longer the ninety-pound weakling of colonial fire departments. It had as many or more engines as Boston and Philadelphia.[194]

As with the watch, the fire department benefited from crucial investments during the 1760s that increased the number of firemen, firehouses, engines and other equipment. When the city council appointed Jacobus Stoutenburgh to succeed Turk in 1761, the number of firemen in the department was still forty-two, the statutory "maximum" set decades earlier, even though the town's population had increased by almost 50 percent. The firemen were equally distributed then—seven in each of the lower wards (none in the Out Ward)—as they had been through the 1750s.

In 1758, the town had purchased four engines, bringing the total to ten. However, there were too few firemen to deploy them all at the same time. It is likely that untrained volunteers acting as ad hoc firefighters on the fireground would assist in the pumping or positioning of the engines. It would take the city a while longer, into the 1760s, to get a fully trained and dedicated department to deploy all the engines.

In the spirit of 1762, as with the enhanced night watch, the provincial assembly empowered the city council to appoint thirty additional firemen to the department.[195] By the end of the year, Jacobus managed seventy-one firemen with the help of two newly appointed "assistants." His official title by that time had been changed from "overseer" to "engineer," reflecting the focus of his technical and maintenance efforts. He was still responsible for maintaining the engines, whether or not they were fully deployed. Of the town's ten engines through the 1760s, about eight (plus or minus one) might have been deployed depending on repair schedules and ad hoc volunteers on the fireground.

However, the placement of firemen was still ward-based—eleven or twelve in each lower ward—even though some wards had more forges, fireplaces, ovens and flammable fixtures than others. Over the next half-dozen years, Jacobus and the city council began molding the department so that it better fit the individual exigencies of each ward. Helpfully, in 1768, the assembly began to appreciate that "there has been an addition to the number of fire engines…and the present firemen are not sufficient to work the same."[196]

The assembly authorized the addition of 45 more firemen, and the department's membership expanded to include 116 men, plus Stoutenburgh and his two assistants. The key difference in its organization, however, was that the firemen were organized by fire company rather than by ward. The larger engines had companies of sixteen to eighteen men, the medium engines had about a dozen men and the small, hand-carried engines had

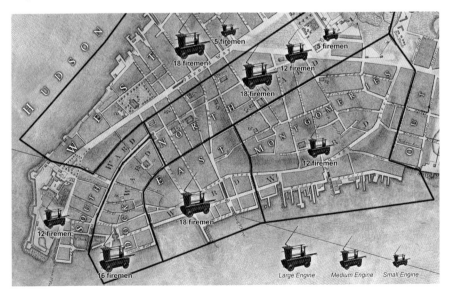

This 1769 map of wards and engines shows the placement of ten fire companies and a little over one hundred firefighters. They were distributed by anticipated need rather than uniformly to each ward (as they were before).

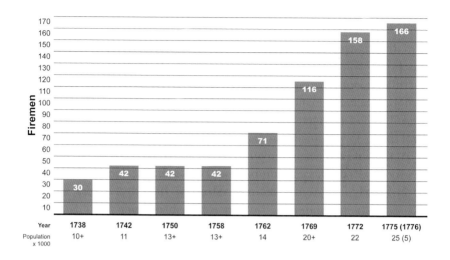

Year	1738	1742	1750	1758	1762	1769	1772	1775 (1776)
Population x 1000	10+	11	13+	13+	14	20+	22	25 (5)

The growth of the FDNY from 1738 to 1776.

five. The complement of engines varied by ward. The West Ward had one large and one small engine. The North Ward had a large engine, a medium engine and a small one. The East and Dock Wards both had large engines. The South and Montgomery Wards had medium engines.[197]

In addition, each engine company then had a foreman, who ensured the readiness of the machines, directed the company from the engine house to the fire and managed the deployment of the machine on the fireground. At fires, each foreman assumed a military-like command, ordering his own men, placing the machines according to the engineer's orders (or, in his absence, to the foreman's best judgment) and monitoring the dedicated civilian brigades. They also cultivated a highly motivated fire company by weeding out members with poor attendance, bad attitudes or noxious habits, like getting drunk.

The organization of the 1769 fire department (an engineer, later chief engineer, and his assistants with foremen and firemen assigned to specific engine companies) would be the essential form of the FDNY for the next century. The department grew from having two engines and no firemen in 1731 to having twelve engine companies and over 160 firemen, all volunteers, in 1775. It was efficient, effective and organizationally structured for growth into the next century. Jacobus Stoutenburgh, as the first "engineer" in America, managed the expanded and streamlined organization with the help of two or three veteran firefighters who were his official "assistants."

The Fires of 1768

The relatively low loss from fire in the period between 1761 and 1775 reinforces the assessment that the New York fire department was experienced and effective, well-managed and well-equipped. During this period, the city regularly increased and upgraded its engines and formed more trained fire companies. In the early 1760s, the city's newspapers, eager to publish a few column inches of text about any calamity, especially a fire, had to settle for a large blaze in London or Boston. They had little to report from New York. A typical fire story, like one in January 1766, rated less than four lines: "A fire broke out in an ash-house, in the yard of Hon. Roger Morris, Esq. of this city, but as soon as the Inhabitants assembled with the engines, they extinguished the same."[198]

However, in later years, like 1768, there were larger fires that warranted more coverage. In March, there were two reports of a fire that was started in Beverly Robinson's stable on Stone Street. One paper reported that the stable was "consumed," as was part of a neighboring kitchen before "the fire was happily subdued, without doing considerable damage."[199] It did mention that high winds "communicated" flames to two warehouses in Pettycoat Lane, one hundred feet or so to the north.

The other newspaper was less placid. It reported: "The flames were already at full height before a bell began to ring."[200] It seemed as though "there was the greatest danger of destruction of that whole quarter of the town." Although it was considerably more alarmed by the possibility of a conflagration, this newspaper reported much the same damage as the other one but added that the roofs of several other houses caught fire and were "much damaged."

Both newspapers, as usual, credited the minimal fire damage to the effective exertions of the "inhabitants." Typically, the papers would also have given the engine companies an appreciative nod, but perhaps for this fire, it was felt to be redundant. It would be obvious to the papers' readers that a fire burning down a couple of buildings, throwing its flames one hundred feet and threatening to burn a quarter of the city needed to be fought with engines—the more the better—to minimize the damage. All could see that the engine companies did their work effectively—the fires, once the alarm was sounded, were quickly and "happily" extinguished.

In 1768, in addition to the Robinson fire, there were several other fires, one of which caused the death of a young child. Mrs. Snead was preparing to wet-nurse a baby in bed, her own two-year-old son asleep beside her,

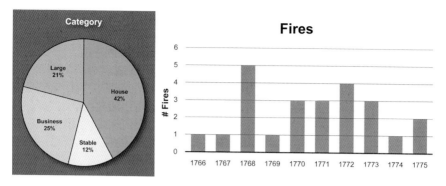

Newsworthy fires (1766–75) by category—large fires in 1768, 1770 and 1772.

when she herself dozed off. The candle burning by the bedside ignited a curtain, which flamed to her bedding and then the rest of the room. Mrs. Snead awoke to escape with burns on her shoulder, and she saved the baby with just a chin burned. Unfortunately, her own child had extensive burns and died the next day.[201]

The other fires in 1768 were without fatality but with some material loss. The stable of Reverend Green partially burned in a fire in which arson was suspected but not confirmed. The bakehouse of one of the Stoutenburgh clan caught on fire, but inhabitants extinguished the fire before there was much damage. A fire destroyed Captain Kennedy's kitchen and damaged several neighboring houses before it was controlled and put out. The captain lost a trunk with £150 in cash and offered a reward of £10 if it was found and returned, no questions asked.[202] Responding, no doubt, to the "rash" of fires, the common council appointed forty-five more firemen, forming nine engine companies. Large fires in 1770 (fifteen buildings) and 1772 (eleven buildings) prompted the next substantial increase in the department in 1772.

FIRE INSURANCE POSTPONED

The largest fire of the period occurred on March 8, 1770. Between 11:00 p.m. and 12:00 a.m. on that Thursday night, a large fire built up in a large, wooden building, St. John's Lodge on Scotch (Ann) Street and remained undiscovered until it broke out with such force that the entire building was consumed in the next twenty minutes. It was a bad spot for a bad fire because it was so far from the rivers, and the local pumps gave little water. The streets were narrow. The houses were made of wood.

The engines "were not half supplied with water for a great part of the time" so that even the "utmost efforts of the inhabitants, greatly assisted by the soldiers in town and the men from His Majesty's ships" could not keep the flames from crossing the street. The fire destroyed sixteen buildings, houses and a few stores before it was contained. There were more houses burned that night than in all the fires of the preceding decade. There was no insurance for the store owners, some of whom lost large inventories, but "most of those who suffered were poor people, several of whom lost their all." A charitable relief fund was set up for the victims "to which…the lieutenant governor and others subscribed liberally." "This is said to be the greatest fire that ever happen'd [sic] in this city."[203]

Shortly after the large March fire, a letter to the editor appeared in the *New-York Gazette-Weekly Post-Boy*, urging the formation of an insurance company. The writer described the system adopted in Philadelphia, in which "gentlemen of property" funded and directed a "contributionship for insuring houses from loss by fire." He then listed thirty-one articles that would form the basis for the society's governance. "The advantages arising from an association of this kind, are too obvious to need being mentioned."[204]

As passionate as the anonymous author of the letter was, he failed in convincing the "gentlemen of property" in New York to emulate Philadelphia's example. Perhaps it was the lack of a big, Boston-size conflagration or the relatively low number of even small fires or the perceived effectiveness of the city's firefighting. It could have been the economic slowdown after the war (1763) that lasted into the 1770s that tipped the scales against novel financial instruments, like fire insurance. Perhaps the city's "gentlemen of property" felt the interest of the public was better served by "subscribing liberally" to charities when a big fire did occur. In any case, the formation of a fire insurance company in New York did not materialize until after the Revolution.

1770s EXPANSION WITH UPGRADES TO ENGINES

While New York tabled the formation of insurance companies before the Revolution, the Common Council of the City of New York was vigilant and decisive. The large fire of 1770, which destroyed as many houses as had been burned in the previous decade, taught the council that conflagrations were possible and dangerous. It was prepared to rapidly expand the fire department where large fires proved to be a likely threat.

For example, in 1772, there was a large fire near St. George's Square, near St. George's Chapel and the intersection of Cherry and Water Streets. Beginning in a distillery late at night and agitated by a wind from the northwest, the fire blazed through and destroyed several houses and warehouse stables on the north side of Water Street before the inhabitants and engines could begin to fight it effectively. It also extended to the south side of Water Street, twice catching the house of Mr. Spring on fire, although, in both, cases these were "happily extinguished." There was also some damage to two houses to the east of where the fire originated.[205] This large fire occurred in early May. The council expanded the fire department, which, by October, had more engines, three dozen more firemen and a fire company near St. George's Square.[206]

City hall continually upgraded the fire engines in the department during the last pre-Revolution decade. Although the common council usually authorized and purchased the engines directly, there were some engines imported or built domestically on speculation in advance of a purchase order. Mr. Shipman merchandised two imported engines, the large one of which he claimed was "superior to any ever sent into these parts…will discharge upwards of 200 gallons per minute."[207] The council purchased one of his large engines in 1772 for a little over £137. The council also purchased two other large engines in 1772, one from Thomas Tiller and the other from Davis Hunt, both from New York.[208]

A year later, George Stanton built and delivered a small engine, the first of three he made in New York. Stanton was one of Jacobus Stoutenburgh's assistant engineers. He had been recently promoted from foreman of the large North Ward engine company. As the department expanded and the city made more organizational demands of Stoutenburgh, Stanton became the principal technician for repairing the fire engines.[209] Stanton delivered his two other engines in 1774, which meant the department, which started with ten engines in 1769, would have had a total of fifteen engines by 1775. However, as the war began in 1776, there were only twelve engine companies, which meant at least three engines were either mothballed or sold.

STOUTENBURGHS: THE NEXT GENERATION

By the 1770s, the city council had also appointed a seven-year veteran, Isaac Stoutenburgh Jr., Jacobus's nephew and Isaac's son, to be one of the assistants to the chief. Isaac Jr. was born in 1738 into circumstances that were more favorable than those his father and uncle, who had lost their father as young children. Not only was Isaac Sr. alive, but he had also prospered as a gunsmith and been elected to the city council by the time he was in his thirties. And although he and his wife, Anneke, had suffered the loss of several children, as was common in those times, Isaac Jr. and two sisters reached adulthood and formed families.

Isaac Sr.'s continuing career as a manager of major public works promoted Isaac Jr.'s education, training and employment. Isaac Jr. trained as a gunsmith, of course, since it was his extended family's trade. By the late 1760s, he had "inherited" the job of maintaining the city's cache of small arms, cleaning and repairing them as well as "mending sundry locks and keys."[210] He had become a fireman during the expansion of the department in 1762 and was then appointed his uncle's assistant in 1769. He would become active in politics in the 1770s—not as his father had in the relative "tranquility" of the fires of 1741 but in the cauldron of a revolution.

Isaac Sr. managed the watch and the city lights through the late 1760s but attended to fewer tasks, such as cleaning and repairing public buildings. He could have been in failing health at the end of 1769, because in early January 1770, he made out his last will and testament. He was dead before the end of January.[211] It is impossible to know if he planned for Jacobus, his brother, or Isaac, his son, to assume the responsibilities of the watch and the city lights, but by the end of the month that followed his death, the common council appointed Jacobus as overseer of the watch, and Isaac began to manage the city lights.[212]

Isaac Stoutenburgh Sr.'s three decades of diligence and hard work that had benefited his family also improved his city. New York's streets were safer, its homes and businesses were more secure and the hazards of the night were better managed. His long tenure in managing the night watch and then expanding and professionalizing it was never easy. In the days of the "volunteer" watch, he had an imperfect cohort of constables, all reluctantly drafted and too poor to pay their way out, who supervised the even-less-motivated, poorer, luckless and unpaid residents, whom many regarded as "drunken snorers." Then, in the professional watch of the 1760s, the tremors of the Revolution began to rattle the peace and quiet enjoyment of the city. It was difficult to decide whether to arrest protesters of the Stamp Act or to join them. Isaac Sr., spared the even more intense conflicts of the 1770s, did his duty as he saw fit for thirty years. America, it seems, has always been blessed with the virtually anonymous but indispensable Isaac Stoutenburghs.

As the city's funding of services continued uninterrupted until the Revolution, Isaac Jr. managed the city lights and was a supplier of oil to the city. Jacobus managed the night watch and the fire department.[213] However, by 1774, with more pressing intensive involvement in politics, Isaac no longer managed the city lights, and Jacobus turned his watch duties over to a new regime.

FDNY JUST BEFORE THE REVOLUTION

Jacobus continued to oversee the growth of the fire department from 1772 to 1776; 1772 had the largest number of fires in the prewar years and, not coincidentally, saw a substantial increase to the size of the fire department in the period following. Even in a year with better fire statistics, a bad fire could still cast a pall over the city. In the last week of December 1773, there was a bad fire in the fort that burned the governor's residence. One person, the governor's fifteen-year-old serving girl, perished in the overwhelming blaze. Governor Tryon, his wife and his daughter barely escaped. The residence itself was destroyed, along with a virtually all the governor's property, including cash, jewelry, furniture, plates, linens, clothing and public and private correspondence.[214] It was then the turn of the populace to offer condolences to a governor, which they did. The provincial assembly reimbursed him £5,000, which is some measure of the scale of the destruction, since a single-family house at the time might cost £500.[215]

Notwithstanding the bad fire in the fort, the scale and frequency of fires in the years before the Revolution seemed to be manageable. The transition from ward-based to engine-based fire companies with foremen made the department more effective. The common council and Jacobus responded to the city's growth by putting firefighting resources closer to higher-risk areas that were likely to need them. Even the Out Ward finally got its own engine.

An advantage Jacobus had in managing the department as it quadrupled in size, from around 40 in 1761 to 160 in 1775, was that it had a stable core of veterans. Even in its large expansion years, like 1769, with the deployment of nine engine companies, and 1772, when two more companies with newer engines were established, there were dozens of firemen who could step up to the responsibilities of foremen or assistant engineers. And as the Revolution rumbled into 1775, the department had over 100 veteran firemen who had served for three or more years; 65 percent (111 firemen) in 1776 were also members in 1772.

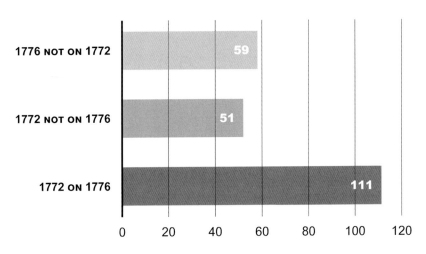

Firemen 1772 vs. 1776

The FDNY before the Revolution, in turbulent times, was stable. Most members of the 1776 FDNY had been members in 1772.

As demonstrated in the bad fires, however, the system had potential weaknesses, such as a late discovery or an insufficient water supply. Discovery depended on a vigilant watch, which, by 1775, was on as professional a basis as it had ever been. Sporadic water delivery would bedevil firefighting into the next century. The common council's first effort to solve the problem was to authorize Christopher Colles in 1774 to build a reservoir in the city to feed pipes through the streets.[216] However, a more significant threat to effective firefighting than a watch or water was the growing social unrest in the American colonies. The complex upheavals of the Revolution would determine the course of firefighting—more specifically, who was doing that firefighting in New York for the next decade.

POLITICAL UPHEAVAL

FDNY UNDER PRESSURE

THE POLITICAL SCENE IN 1775 NEW YORK

The New York fire department was a political creation authorized by an act of the provincial assembly and implemented by the Common Council.[217] The assembly determined the maximum number of firemen and their duties, exemptions and privileges. The council appointed the firemen and recorded each fireman's name in its minutes. When a fireman left the department on his own or through the efforts of others, the council replaced them by appointment and made a formal written entry in the minutes.

As the Revolution began, what governmental agency was in charge, and how they enforced their authority was quite fluid and confusing. This muddle eventually spanned all levels of government from the provincial assembly to the lamp lighters, with the firemen and their duties, exemptions and privileges somewhere in between. At least the marginalization of the provincial assembly occurred in early April 1775 and was unambiguous.

By 1775, the Revolutionary factions in New York included a mix of some "elite," like John Jay, a wealthy King's College (later Columbia)–educated lawyer. Other leaders were newly moneyed, like Isaac Sears, who enjoyed success as a privateer and became a leader of the Sons of Liberty. Many laborers, carpenters, sailmakers, coopers and other craftsmen influenced events through an association called the Mechanics Committee.

These factions jostled for control of the Revolutionary agenda, with the moderate elite generally favoring a more reconciliatory policy toward Britain. When the time came to send five delegates to an all-colony congress in

Philadelphia, the moderates selected members from their more conservative faction. The Mechanics proposed a different slate, resulting in three weeks of edgy negotiations. The elite finally prevailed to keep their slate of delegates, but they promised to support a nonimportation agreement—essentially a boycott of British goods—if such a policy were adopted at the congress.[218]

Perhaps to the dismay of a New York delegate or two, this congress did endorse a nonimportation plan in the fall of 1774, first by approving and supporting the Suffolk Resolves. The resolves were the response in Massachusetts to the punitive British "Massachusetts Government Act" that had effectively revoked the colony's 1691 charter.[219] They included a boycott of British goods, the establishment of an alternative government and a call to raise a militia to oppose British military forces.

Even more directly, the same congress "recommended" each colony implement the "association," the agency by which Revolutionary committees would enforce boycotts of British goods and restrict American shipments to Britain. Moderates may still have had hopes for reconciliation, but "no sane man could doubt that…congress had assumed the powers of government and counseled rebellion."[220] The plan of the congress was to arrogate substantial governmental authority from the British regime to its Revolutionary committees, such as the Committees of Inspection.

The elite and the Mechanics had formed the "Committee of Sixty," which shared power between the two factions. In early 1775, this committee proposed province-wide conventions to select New York delegates to a Second Continental Congress, where every colony would again send delegates. If there were any possibility that the provincial assembly or governor could stop the momentum of this movement, they needed to act quickly and deliberately.

But the Committee of Inspection, Mechanics Committee and Sons of Liberty had done their job in garnering popular support and intimidating Loyalists, those colonists who still supported the British regime. When the congressional delegation finally emerged on April 20, 1775, the provincial assembly did not effectively oppose it. New York's colonial legislature, for almost a century the provincial assembly, essentially melted into irrelevance.[221]

FIREMEN AND THE SONS OF LIBERTY

When the news of the Battles of Lexington and Concord struck New York, the Sons of Liberty emptied two ships of cargo intended for British troops in Boston. One of their leaders, Marinus Willett, then took a contingent

Marinus Willett was a prominent colonel in Washington's army. As a leader of the Sons of Liberty, he sought pretexts to burn Loyalist property, which inevitably led to tensions with firemen.

to city hall to demand the muskets and other military supplies that the city had, for decades, stored to enable a rapid expansion of its citizen militia to resist raids or invasions.[222] Historians have noted the seizure, as it was a highly visible example of the radical tide in April 1775 rolling New York toward revolution.

Jacobus Stoutenburgh, on the other hand, although he was a patriot, was not so keen on the forcible removal of the city's weaponry by the Willett contingent. Jacobus was a gunsmith as well as the chief fire engineer, and the weapons had been entrusted to his care and maintenance, as they had been to his brother, Isaac, before him. His report of the seizure did not have the ring of approval in it one would expect of a solid supporter of the Sons of Liberty.

> *I, Jacobus Stoutenburgh, do hereby certify that there were five hundred and twenty-two muskets [sic] belonging to the Corporation of the City of New York and under my care in the city hall when the account of the Lexington Battle arrived and were taken away from thence by sundry persons....*

And I do further certify that twenty-eight musquets [sic] *more, which also belonged to the corporation and were given to Mr. Isaac Stoutenburgh to clean &c were taken away from him and that each of the said musquets* [sic] *with the accoutrements is well worth three pounds, five shillings, and I also further certify that at the same time six iron bullet moulds were also taken away from the city hall.*
—*Jacobus Stoutenburgh, New York, September 6th, 1775*[223]

The extended Stoutenburgh family supported the Patriotic cause and the Revolution. Jacobus's nephew Isaac helped raise a battalion of volunteers for the New York militia. There were at least ten "upstate" Stoutenburghs in the Dutchess County militia, several of whom were officers. However, the incident of turning over the city weapons to the "sundry persons" illustrates that the support of the Revolution was far from monolithic. The politics and sentiments of the Sons of Liberty were not identical to those of Jacobus Stoutenburgh, nor did they always resonate with the firemen of New York.

The "social class" of the two groups could explain part of this discord. Superficially, the class of the Sons of Liberty might seem to be more or less the same as the class of the firemen. There was, of course, some overlap in occupations; for example, carpenters, coopers and sailmakers were in both groups. But to be a fireman, a male resident of the city had to be a "freeman" (or a "freeholder," essentially a class of freeman with substantial, real property), an important civic distinction in the body politic. Freemen in colonial New York paid a fee to "register" with the city, which allowed them certain privileges, such as working in a trade or craft, and obligated them to perform civic duties, such as serving on juries.

Although New York was as broadly participative as any other American city, not every White male resident was a freeman, including many of those in the Sons of Liberty/Mechanics faction. That difference had generated conflict in the 1774 negotiations, forming the early Revolutionary committees. Isaac Sears, a leader of the Sons of Liberty/Mechanics faction, argued for voting rights for "everyman whose liberties were concerned," while the elite/moderate faction favored voting by "none but the freeholders and freemen."[224]

More than just a few civic distinctions separated firemen from the Revolutionary radicals. Firemen had risked their lives to preserve life and property in New York for the previous forty years and continued to do so as the Revolution began to boil. The Sons of Liberty had no such predisposition. It was more than just the ill-fated tea that the Sons were

Developing the "Modern" Colonial FDNY (1740–75)

prepared to destroy. They were ready to wreak a little havoc on the property of any official, merchant, printer or other Loyalist who supported the British regime. To them, burning Loyalist pamphlets in large bonfires seemed like an altogether good idea. In mid-1775, a band of Isaac Sears-led radicals, profoundly unsympathetic to notions of a free press, destroyed the machines of Loyalist printer James Rivington.[225] When the Sons burned Loyalist pamphlets, effigies or businesses, it was still the job of the firemen to keep the havoc from getting out of control.

FIREMEN AND THE ELITE: THE PLIGHT OF JOHN DASH

Pressured by the Sons, the firemen also experienced pressure of a different kind from the elite, who, by the summer of 1775, had formed a provincial congress for New York and were enthusiastically filling the vacuum left by the pro-British provincial assembly. They were making things increasingly difficult for Loyalists or anyone else who might be an "enemy of liberties of America," which, by their account, included anyone who opposed their authority. Particularly active was their Committee of Safety, which sought to disarm, detain, dispossess and/or banish political opponents. On the congress's list of institutions that needed modest renovation was the fire department. Of course, even before it "perfected" the department as a whole, it had in its sights those firemen who might have been Loyalists. The plight of John Balthasar Dash, one of Stoutenburgh's assistants, illustrated the ways and means of the Committee of Safety.

John Balthasar Dash first appeared on the rolls of the fire department in 1772, when he was a member of the West Ward Engine Company.[226] He was a tinsmith, a craft that, at the time, produced innumerable household objects, such as coffee pots, ovens, snuff boxes, toys, shoe buckles and lanterns. Tinsmiths often worked in other metals, such as copper and lead, to extend their product lines. He learned his trade in Germany before immigrating to New York in the 1750s.[227] By 1760, Dash was making stoves and ovens for the city workhouse.[228] By 1765, he was advertising shoe buckles and Philadelphia buttons in the *New-York Gazette*.[229] And by the 1770s, he was making and maintaining the city's public lamps.[230]

His son, John Balthasar Jr., born in 1755, later joined his father to expand the family business and followed in his father's footsteps by joining the fire department.[231] The father and son also became charter members of the German Society, dedicated to helping German immigrants, especially impoverished ones, make a go of it in their new country.[232] In addition, the Dash family participated in fundraising for the Lutheran church.[233]

How did John Dash, a sober fireman, skilled tinsmith, solid family man and modest philanthropist, become a target for the Committee of Safety? He might have caught their notice as early as 1770. Due to an earlier successful boycott of British goods to protest the then-new Townshend taxes, the value of British imports to New York declined from £482,000 in 1769 to £72,000 in 1770.[234] Beleaguered British merchants urged Parliament to remove the tax barriers to trade, which it did on all but tea in 1770. Parliament thereby maintained the principal of its authority to tax without putting any substantive commerce at risk. The merchants of New York were satisfied with the reversal of the tax policy, such as it was, and felt that the boycott had served its purpose and should be lifted. They desperately needed to rebuild their businesses. Many were on the verge of bankruptcy.

The Sons of Liberty were of a more "all-or-nothing" mindset. They argued that unless the tax on tea was also lifted, America would be vulnerable to future taxes and impositions on their liberties. They still adamantly supported a general nonimportation boycott. However, a supplement to a July 1770 issue of the *New-York Gazette* reported, "'That the sense of our inhabitants has been again taken,'...and that there appear'd [*sic*] 'a great majority for importing everything except such articles as are...subject to duty.'"[235] A large majority in the city wanted the return of commerce, jobs and a more robust economy, regardless of the vestigial tea tax. The Sons of Liberty would, as a practical matter, acquiesce to the growing and dominant sentiment to import, but that did not mean they had to go away quietly.

While the supplement began with a simple assessment of the mood of city, what followed was a portent of how the Sons, the Committees of Inspection/Safety and other factions that favored an all-out boycott of British imports would operate in the Revolutionary future. Following the report of "the sense of the inhabitants" was a list of residents who were in favor of the proposal to import. The list was printed on two full supplemental pages in the *Gazette*. The "editorial" note attached said that they had advertised the names of these pro-import people in the newspaper so the public could "justly discriminate between those who have had a due regard to the liberties of their country and those who have not so well attended to them." (There is a partial list here; the complete list can be found at https://www.savingny.com/appendix20.html).

Imagine the dismay of the men and women whose names suddenly appeared in the largest circulation newspaper in the city, stigmatized as a

To the PUBLIC.

AS the late letter of our committee of inspection, to the Merchants committee in Philadelphia, asserts, ",That the sense of our inhabitants' "had been again taken," concerning the non-importation agreement, and that there appear'd " a great " majority for importing every thing except such ar- " ticles as are or may hereafter be subject to duty, for the purpose of raising a revenue in America " The friends to the non-Importation agreement, submit the matter to the public; as the most proper judges in a case which concerns American liberty in general ; not doubting, that in their determination they will justly discriminate between those who have had a due regard to the liberties of their country, and those who have not so well attended to them as the importance of the subject justly requires.

FOR IMPORTING.

A	
ANderson Elias, jun.	Bache Theophilact,
Aptell William,	Beekman Gerrard, Wm
Anderson George,	Bleeker Anthony L. *V. Ma.*
Anderson Nicholas,	Brownjohn Thomas, *Drug.*
Allen William, N.	Beekman Henry;
Anthony Nicholas N.	Burl Robert,
Angle Henry;	Baker Robert,
Anderson John,	Byvanck William,
Adams John,	Brewerton George, Esq;
Anthony Nicholas, ffen.	Boots Andrew,
Anthony Thephilus,	Bavin William,
Atwood Thomas B. *druge.*	Blanck Isaac,
	Brown John,

A partial list of about eight hundred colonists who favored imports were publicly attacked in a major newspaper in 1770. The complete list included thirty-three firemen.

suspicious group who had "not so well attended to" the liberties of their country. Moreover, the list had consequences for the future of firefighting during the Revolution. About 25 percent of the members of the 1771 fire department (thirty-three) were also on that inflammatory list.[236]

The fact that John B. Dash was on this list was not surprising, given that he was a tinsmith and relied on the import of tin and other metals for his livelihood. He would have been "for importation." Most of the other eight hundred on the list were similarly merchants, importers, tradesmen and shopkeepers, all of whom made their living with finished British goods or other imported materials. Eight hundred was not that many, according to the Sons—just a small fraction of the twenty thousand people in the city. Even that small number included many women, "who, from their sex… were not intitled to declare their sense of the question." Why the Sons insisted on publishing the names of women who were not "intitled," they did not explain.

The Sons of Liberty/Committee of Safety no doubt approached John Dash in the winter of 1775–76. They were looking to propagate "the association" throughout the province, especially to prominent citizens in New York, like Dash. The association was a formal endorsement of the program of the first two continental congresses that included a renewal of nonimportation and nonconsumption policies on all British goods. It also included a non-export policy on American products, with a few exceptions, to Britain and its territories.

Agreeing to join the association also meant that one accepted and supported the authority of the continental congress and the local Revolutionary committees. And, of course, by supporting congress, a member of the association would be expected to oppose any representation of British rule, be it civil or military, ministerial Britain or Loyalist American. Dash was more than prominent enough for a visit from the committee. He was a foreman in the fire department, a supplier of lanterns and other finished metal products to the city and a leader in the German community.

It is hard to imagine that John Dash would be an "early adopter" of the association. He was on the record as being against nonimportation, and he was unlikely to seek political guidance from his antagonists, the local Sons of Liberty. In fact, although he did remain with the fire department, his clear identification as a "nonassociator," placed him in the path of repression from the new revolutionary regime.

In the spring of 1776, Dash was among the almost sixty "disaffected persons" in New York City who had their personal firearms and other weapons confiscated. The list of weapons was short, less than eighty weapons with an "appraised" valued of about £203. Dash had a blunderbuss and two pistols taken from him. Garret Abeel, the chairman of the committee in charge of the commandeered weapons, made a point to record: "None or very few of the arms &c mentioned in this list are fit for immediate service."[237]

The Revolutionary committees redoubled their efforts in May 1776 to control the potentially militant Loyalists by directly arresting those who they thought would not respond to a summons. Luckily, Dash was in the group of "suspected persons" in the city who the committee felt would answer their summons. Still, he was on a very short and very conspicuous list.[238]

Within a month, on June 15, 1776, yet another Revolutionary committee, the Committee to Detect Conspiracies, produced a more comprehensive list of "disaffected persons and those of equivocal character." It included the last royal governor, Tryon; a Delancy; an Apthorp; a couple of Bayards; and a few Crugers, the elite of the Loyalists, many of whom had already

John Jay was the president of the Second Continental Congress and, later, the first U.S. chief justice. As a Revolutionary leader, he curtailed firemen's militia exemptions and prosecuted prominent Loyalist firemen.

left town. At least Dash was in good company on this "list of suspected persons." On the negative side, the committee had marked him not only to be summoned but also definitely arrested.[239]

The conspiracy committee itself had a higher pedigree than most local revolutionary agencies, as it included Philip Livingston, who would sign the Declaration of Independence (albeit a little after July 4); John Jay, who had already served as the president of the Second Continental Congress, would become the first chief justice of the supreme court and direct U.S. foreign policy in the 1780s; and Gouverneur Morris, a founding father who would write the preamble to the U.S. Constitution. It is unlikely that John Dash fully valued the caliber of the committee that was intent on arresting him.

Dash was never arrested. The judicial process itself became a bottleneck when processing all the accused Loyalists. There was no infrastructure large enough to execute all the summons and arrests the committee issued. Loyalists were paroled, exiled to Connecticut and jailed. "But the slow-moving processes of the judicial committees were altogether insufficient" for the full scale of the task.[240] Most Loyalists were still at-large when, two weeks later, the British sailed into New York Harbor and landed on Staten Island. The provincial congress and the Committees of Safety/Conspiracy retired to White Plains. Dash was safe in New York.

The Provincial Congress Reforms the Fire Department

In the first few months of 1776, the fire department was in a state of flux. The New York Provincial Congress had almost ensured some confusion a year earlier when it subtly attempted to change the terms of the firemen's service. Perhaps zealous members of the Sons of Liberty had analyzed the "supplement" list five years before to discover the thirty-plus firemen in favor of importation. More likely, the Sons had so often bumped into the firemen responding to Revolutionary blazes that they realized not all firemen shared their enthusiasm for a good bonfire of Loyalist furniture and fixtures. In any case, the mood of the congress was to redirect the firemen to their own congressional purposes, one of which was to raise and organize substantial military forces.

At first glance, the September 2, 1775 resolution of the provincial congress seemed to affirm the firemen's long-standing exemption from militia duty: "That the firemen of the City of New York be, and they are, hereby exempted from the military night watch and being called upon as minute-men or of the militia to go out of the city."[241] The firemen, however, clearly saw the loophole in the measure. Although they were exempt from militia duty outside the city, by deliberate and somewhat devious congressional omission, they were no longer exempt from militia duty inside the city. "As the duties of a militia-man within the city at that time, were exceedingly burdensome, especially to those tradesmen and mechanics and workingmen who continued to reside there, the resident firemen were evidently alarmed by that seeming intention to violate those rights and exemptions."[242]

In response, six days later, the firemen submitted a petition to the provincial congress. "To the honorable congress....We, the firemen of the City of New York...cannot serve two masters to draw out in the milletery [sic] service & to tend our fire engines." They asked for their historical exemption and acknowledged their duty, which was to muster with fellow city residents in the case of invasion. If that were not "agreeable to the honourable [sic] congress, we must lay down firemen ship and turn out as sholdjers [sic]."[243] The leaders of the FDNY who signed the petition represented a broad political spectrum—from proto-Loyalists, like George Stanton, to Patriot supporters of the new order, like William J. Elsworth, both longtime veterans of New York firefighting.

The Committee of Safety, then managing many of these details for the congress in the city, chose to ignore the substance of the petition. Instead, they directed: "That a copy of a resolution of the provincial congress, which exempts the firemen from certain military duty, should be served on one of the memorialists."[244] Of course, the firemen had already seen the resolution, which is the reason they presented the petition in the first place. The committee's posture may have seemed perfunctory to some, but it spoke loud and clear to the firemen. They began to make their own individual decisions about whether to continue as firemen, join the military or get out of town.

THE 1776 LIST OF FIREMEN

Although there is no official fire department list in the *1775–76 Minutes of the Common Council*, a roster of firemen from 1776 does exist, anonymous and undated. John Dash was still listed as a member in good standing, which would place the formation of the list before May, when his summons was on its way—maybe even before March, when he had his weapons confiscated. In any case, probably in the spring of 1776, an official agency took a census of firemen and recorded the results in an unusual form.[245]

The usual common council lists, such as the one in 1772, first recorded the department management with Stoutenburgh and his assistants and then the engine companies with the names of the foreman and firemen assigned to each company. With the exception of Stoutenburgh, this odd 1776 list had no reference to the management, no listing of engine companies, no foremen and no assignment of the firemen to any particular engine. Whoever made up this list was not that interested in the organizational details of a functioning fire department. They were much more interested in tracking the individuals of the fire department and putting them in categories, as shown in the partial list here. (See the full list and references at https://www.savingny.com/appendix21.html.)

There were several military categories that roughly represented the Continental army; the "state" militia, or minutemen; and the city militia. The military categories had thirty-four names. There was another category labeled "out of town" with thirty-one names. The largest category, "firemen in town," had a little over one hundred names. Essentially, whatever agency composed this 1776 list provided a "snapshot" of the members of the fire department in the spring of 1776. The names in the categories reflected the decisions the firemen had been making since the previous September—to join the military, to get out of town or to remain firemen.

Firemen of New York.

[Miscel. Pap. 34 : 223.]

The List of firemen of the City of New York under the Command of Jacobus Stoutenburgh Engenier. 1776.

Philip Brasher, Adgutent of the first batteleon.
George January, Capt in a beat.
Victors Bickers, Leift in the Contenantel.
Cornelus Bickers, Leift in the Contenantel.
Jonathan Black, Leift in the second battellon.
John Stegh, Leift in the second battellon.
John Walter, Leift in a beat.
Lewis tiebou, in the first battellon privet.

Garret waldron,	John hoogeland,	thomas Lawrence,
Peter G. waldron,	John montanie,	Jacob Brower,
John silvester,	timothy Rushel,	John Brower,
Jacob Brower,	William Eagles,	John Bortine,
Henry Van Winckelen,	issac Bokea,	John Miltenburger,
James Kip,	David moris,	anthony post,
James M'Cullen,	Robert Berry,	John tergay.
Joseph Baldwin,	Jacob moris,	

These belongs all to the first and second battalien.

John Somerndyck,   Gerit Peterson,   henry Shut.

These three belongs to the Light horse.

fredrick Bard,	John Bogert,	Barent Christopher,
anthony King,	Jacobus Quick,	Robert thomson,
Joseph person,	Jacob Bowler,	Nathan horton,
aaron Bancker,	Henry Relay,	abram warner,
moris Earle,	isaac van Deursen,	Lancaster burling,
Berard weecks,	michal garit,	andrew ten Eyck,
Benjamin Carpenter,	henry sickels,	Gerardus Burger,
henry Bogert,	Peter Roome,	Lawrence hartwick,
thomas maridet,	thomas Burling,	John Class,
James van seys,	Ellick Miller,	Garet stymets.
abram Rushell,		

[These is all out of town.]

Firemen in town.

Isaac Marshalck,	Gerardus smith,	Cornelus swartwout,
Edward Doughty, Se'	Charles miller,	henry thomas,
isaac Labagh,	Chales Phillips,	william vermillie,
John Gillilan,	Daniel ten Eyck,	James Barrow,
John Burns,	henry sickels,	John Barrow,
Theop' hardenbroeck,	Evert wessels,	John van torne,
matice vreedenburgh,	John silvester,	henry outenbergh,
Elias De Grushe,	Richard ten Eyck,	Peter bogert,
matice warner,	Jacob Smith,	francis Bassett,
henry Riker,	Jacob Norris,	Jeronemis alstyne,
norman tolmie,	Joseph Cox,	william pears,
andrew Riker,	thomas Burns,	william Bockay,
John Stout,	John Russel,	william post,
George fisher,	timothy wood,	william Elsworth,
william Carman,	abram van Dusen,	Nathan fish,
Richard heyer,	George Arthart,	John fish,
thomas warner,	Isaac Meed,	John young,
francis Dominick,	francis post,	James Lickletter,
David henry mellows,	Jacob vervalen,	Christopher Dicking,
Valentine arnell,	Peter wilse,	wendel De Boos,

The 1776 list of firemen (partial).

Although the author of the 1776 list is not known, the New York Provincial Congress would find a list of this kind quite useful when fulfilling one of its most important mandates: to raise an army. During the Revolution, the provincial congress, later the state assembly, would raise and organize tens of thousands of troops for the state militia and Washington's Continental army. By the end of the war, New York had raised, organized and supplied over fifty thousand troops.[246]

There was always pressure on the provincial congress to provide more troops. They raised the upper age limit for mandatory military duty from fifty to sixty during the war. The lower age limit remained sixteen. They imposed fines and imprisonment for those who refused to serve.[247] It is little wonder that the provincial congress would look at the 1776 list and count over one hundred firemen who had no specifically designated military assignment before the anticipated invasion. If put into service, the firemen could fill an entire infantry company.

In June 1776, the provincial congress felt it was necessary to fine-tune its policy for firemen. "That such of the firemen be exempted as will agree to form a separate company for the preservation of the city, in case of invasion, and to be under the command of the general, until the further order of this congress."[248] While this resolution seemed to recognize the efforts already made by the firemen to train as militia, its oblique language changed what was to happen in case of an invasion. The general who was referred to but remained unnamed was Washington. When the invasion came, the firemen would be under Washington's command; they would be part of Washington's Continental army.

Being part of the Continental army would oblige the firemen to fight anywhere in America, even as far south as North Carolina or Georgia, with an enlistment period much longer than those of men in a militia. This was a far more austere proposition for the firemen than being included in a city or state militia. In the militia, they would at least be fighting somewhere close to home in New York and for weeks or months rather than the duration of the war. As a result of this new policy, the firemen continued to make their decisions: stay, enlist or exit.

The next month, the Committee of Safety had to reverse this policy. A July 13, 1776 order published in the newspaper by the secretary of the committee stated: "The members of the different fire engine companies that remain in this city ought not to be called out to military duty." The foremen of the companies were to engage as many as necessary to fill the vacancies of those who "entered in continental service or have removed out of town."[249] But it may have been too late to influence the course of events. In another month, the shooting would start, which would throw into sharp relief the decision each fireman would have to make for themselves.

THE IMMINENT BRITISH INVASION: FINAL CHOICES

In 1776, Washington shifted his army down from Boston to New York and prepared to defend Manhattan against the anticipated return of the British army. As the Continental troops moved into town, the residents continued their exodus. Only five thousand residents remained from the city's prewar population of twenty-five thousand. New York became less of a bustling commercial city and more of a military garrison. The city was under the uneasy combined governance of the Revolutionary committees and Washington's army. But by the end of June, the provincial congress and its committees had moved north when the British fleet arrived. Only Washington's army and a few thousand intrepid residents remained in Manhattan.

With the British returning and the influence of the Committee of Safety waning, the firemen would soon have another choice, one that had been suppressed by the pressure of the Revolutionary committees. The firemen would have the option to join the British to support the Loyalist cause, which could include enlisting in Loyalist militia units to fight in and around New York.

When a society convulses in revolution, the adversaries often begin making lists—lists of the good guys and lists of the bad guys. The New York Provincial Congress began making their lists of Loyalists, their bad guys, in 1775, with the people they singled out to disarm and, later, those they summoned to arrest. Loyalists listed their good guys in their militia lists. But the most important list, the list that confirmed Loyalism with virtual certainty, was the "address" that Loyalists signed after the Continental army had been pushed out of Manhattan and the British army was in complete control.

The Loyalists submitted their "address," essentially a manifesto, to General William Howe, the commander of the British forces in America and his brother Admiral Richard Howe. The Howes had just directed the almost flawless campaign that drove Washington's army off Long Island and then out of Manhattan. The Loyalist manifesto proclaimed their allegiance to King George III, their esteem for the British "constitution" and their wish to restore New York to "His Majesty's protection and peace."[250] A list followed the "address" with about 1,600 signatures.

The manifesto was a succinct statement of what Loyalists believed and why they were choosing to stay in New York until the Revolution was over. The signers included those who had been threatened by the Sons of Liberty or even proscribed by the several congressional committees; those who had not been threatened but disapproved of what they considered to be "illegal" acts, such as the destruction of newspapers; those who saw profit in providing supplies to the British as they had in the last war; those who needed licenses or other governmental approval to stay in business; and those who wanted to live as they always had without having to sign on to one militia or another. Since estimates say only 5,000 civilians remained in New York at this time, early October 1776, the 1,600 Loyalists must have included a remarkably high proportion of the householders who stayed.

With the preponderance of Loyalists in the city, it is not surprising that of five of them, John Dash, George Stanton, Francis Dominick, Jeronimus Alstine and George Waldegrove, assistants or foreman before the war, became the leadership of the FDNY during the Revolution. They were the core that emerged in late 1776 to continue the FDNY's mission of keeping New York safe, which would turn out to not be a simple task. They all signed the Loyalist address in 1776. Their sentiments were public knowledge since they were listed in the Sons of Liberty's supplement advertisement in 1770. They may not have been right, but at least they were consistent.

Since the Patriot militias were strewn outside the city and those in Washington's army were rarely near New York, none in the Patriot military did any firefighting in the city during the war. A comparison of the 1776 list to the lists of those who served in the Patriot military during the Revolution puts the number of firemen in the Patriot military at about fifty-five. Comparing the 1776 list of firemen to the list of Loyalists puts the number of Loyalist firemen at about twenty-one. Their contributions would be essential for an effective FDNY during the war, but they were not enough by themselves to adequately protect the city. Yet someone kept the city from burning down.

Of the firemen who do not appear on the Loyalist or military lists, some left town (out-of-town, unlisted), and others stayed (in-town, unlisted). The estimate of the in-town category is important, because the Loyalists needed the support of their "unaffiliated" colleagues who were still in the city to deploy enough engines to effectively fight fires. The estimate here places about seventy to eighty unaffiliated firemen in the city. (See http://www.savingny.com/appendix22.html for estimates and comparisons of lists.)

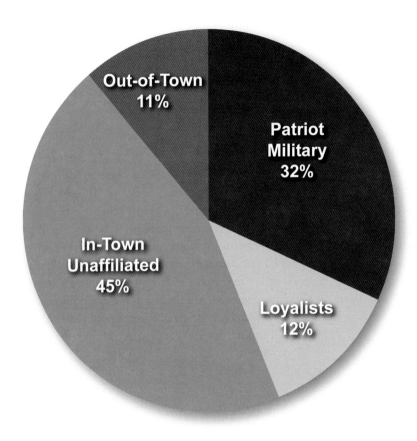

The FDNY during the Revolution could draw from about ninety veterans who were still in town.

The graph above, with data from 1776, does not represent the composition of the FDNY during the entire war, since "out-of-towners," like Peter Roome and Jacobus Quick came back into the city while others left. In addition, other people stepped into the firefighting role. When the department formed a new engine company in 1780, during the middle of the war, veteran Daniel Ten Eyck became its foreman. Other veteran members included Charles Phillips, who was still "in town," along with Loyalists Thomas Barrow and Evert Wessels. But it also had over a dozen new members who had never been on the rolls of the department.[251]

Analyzing the probable disposition of the firemen at the beginning of the war, however imprecise, does demonstrate one certainty: the firemen did not all enlist in the Patriot military or leave the city. Some stayed and fought fires. The FDNY, as with the rest of New York's populace, was in flux during the Revolution. Some firemen returned after initially leaving the city. Others headed in the opposite direction. But at no time did the firefighters of New York, even under the most trying times of the revolution, leave the city completely undefended.

However, to defend the city from fire during the war was always difficult and often dangerous to both the firefighters and other civilians in the city. The department moved from civilian governance to British martial law and then to a hybrid of civilian/military control. How the department navigated these unchartered transitions to fulfill its firefighting mission is recounted in the following chapters.

Part Three

THE FDNY AND
THE REVOLUTION (1775—83)

A view from Wall Street and Broadway: Trinity Church, circa 1776 (*right*); Lutheran Church (*left*); the schoolhouse can be seen down the slope that leads to the Hudson River.

THE GREAT NEW YORK FIRE OF 1776

NEW YORK IN THE SUMMER OF '76

As the tumult of the Revolution rumbled into New York in the early summer of 1776, the fire department was still relatively intact. It is true that a dozen or so Loyalist firemen would not have to be paranoid to think someone was out to get them—the committees of congress were. It might also have been true that congressional sophistry on firemen's exemptions persuaded more than a few to exit the city. But, until May, the bulk of the department was functional and looked to the city council for its civil leadership.

Then, in May, the city council adjourned—for the next seven years. In June, the provincial government, with its controlling committees, moved north to White Plains, curtailing its influence in the city. By July, amid Washington's army, the fire department was operating more by professional instinct than civil direction. In August, after two months of provocative lethargy, Britain's General Howe sent forces to Brooklyn, outflanked the Americans there and forced Washington's army back to Manhattan. In September, the British executed a textbook-perfect amphibious landing from the East River that convinced Washington to evacuate lower Manhattan for defensive lines prepared to the north, in the heights of Harlem.

Washington and his generals had foreseen the difficulty of defending lower Manhattan. British naval power overwhelmingly dominated the harbor and rivers surrounding the city. They could attack virtually anywhere, at any time. The question naturally arose of what should be done with the city in

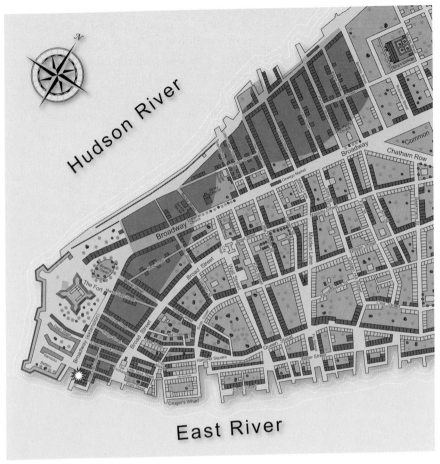

The great fire of 1776 began near the southern tip of the city and spread rapidly north, consuming blocks of buildings every hour.

the quite probable circumstance of withdrawing American forces. General Nathanael Greene articulated one strategy: "I give it as my oppinion [*sic*] that a general and speedy retreat is absolutely necessary….I would burn the city & subburbs [*sic*]."[252]

Washington, of course, understood the strategic importance of not getting trapped in Manhattan. Although he could also see both the pros and cons of torching the city, he himself favored Nathanial Greene's strategy: "Had I been left to the dictates of my own judgment, New York should have been laid in ashes before I quitted it."[253] However, with remarkable deference to congress, he asked for its direction. "If we should be obliged to abandon this town, ought it to stand as winter quarters for the enemy? They would derive great conveniences from it on the one hand—and much property would be destroyed on the other—it is an important question but will admit of but little time for deliberation."[254]

There were good reasons, both practical and political, for Americans to not burn themselves out of their own cities. Congress tended to the practical: "The congress would have especial care taken…that no damage be done to the said city by…[Washington's] troops on their leaving it; the congress having no doubt of being able to recover the same, tho [*sic*] the enemy should for a time obtain possession of it."[255] Congress took the long view. This vast military apparatus of the remote king that was about to take over New York would be gone sooner or later. America would prevail, and when it did, Congress wanted its cities still standing.

The politics were clear. To get the broadest support from the American people, congress did not want to authorize or encourage American forces to burn down American cities, as the British had already done in 1775 to Charlestown (next to Boston) and Falmouth, Maine. Americans who identified with their burned-out compatriots surely resented this blunt British instrument of war. Moreover, in New York, large fires would inevitably destroy the property of pro-Revolution Patriots. Even if two-thirds of the city belonged to Loyalists as General Greene roughly estimated, that meant the other third at least might be Patriots. Congress did not want to lose the sympathy and support of several thousand Patriot families, many of whom, unlike their Loyalist neighbors, had left the city and could not protect their property.

Washington followed the resolutions of congress to the letter, but his ability to prevent destruction in the city was limited. The rank-and-file of the army, especially the troops from New England, according to some accounts, wanted to burn down the town. Letters from English officers on Long Island reported: "I have just heard that there has been a most dreadful fray in New York. The New Englanders insisted on setting the town on fire and retreating; this was opposed by the New Yorkers…and a battle has been the consequence in which many lost their lives." And another: "Deserters tell us they are in great confusion at New York, one party wanting to burn the town, and the other to save it."[256]

Samuel Bayard, a prominent New York Loyalist, swore under oath that he had been told by an American captain named Bowman that he and his artillery company had put out fires set in houses on Pearl Street just a few days before the battle on Long Island. And later, his company had been "up the greatest part of the night to prevent one Capt. Forster's company from setting the city on fire." Also, according to Bayard, a New Yorker he knew quite well, Joseph Smith, threatened to burn down Bayard's house rather than allow it to be used by British troops.[257]

Washington followed the congressional resolution to not damage the city and was committed to "take every measure in my power to prevent it."[258] But when he moved with his army north to Harlem, his orders became mere suggestions. There were substantial numbers of people beyond his control—New York civilians, like Joseph Smith, and a few of the Sons of Liberty, soldiers like those in Captain Forster's company, militiamen who blended quickly into the populace as the British took over, sailors assigned to build and arm fireships and several officers, often lieutenants and captains, all of whom saw, as did Nathanael Greene, the military advantages resulting from the destruction of the city.[259]

The Fire Department in August 1776

Many firemen, including Chief Jacobus Stoutenburgh, retreated with Washington. About a third of the firemen had already enlisted in the Continental army or state militias. With the British takeover of Manhattan, other firemen were motivated to join the Patriot military. Some became auxiliaries for transport and supply lines, including the preparation and repair of guns, Stoutenburgh's most likely role.[260] More firemen also joined those already "out-of-town," motivated, no doubt, like their earlier colleagues to avoid living in or near a war zone. It would be reasonable to estimate, based on where the firemen were in the spring of 1776, that by the end of 1776, less than half of them, perhaps eighty or so, were still in the city.

Loyalist firemen were still in the city and planned to remain. Their leaders included John B. Dash, George Stanton, Francis Dominick, Jeronimus Alstine and George Waldegrove. They had been foremen of engine companies in the prewar department. Dash and Stanton also served as assistants to Stoutenburgh. As foremen, they all could maintain the engines and other firefighting equipment and manage the fire companies and bucket brigades at a fire. Stanton and Dash had extensive experience in repairing engines. Stanton, as noted earlier, had even built several of the engines used by the city. Dash had also built and maintained the city lamps for many years. As the British and their German mercenaries streamed into New York, General Robertson, the British officer in charge of the civilian governance of the city, appointed Dash to supervise the twelve engines in use at that time, maintain the city lamps and look after the Sandy Hook Lighthouse.[261]

However, as the British marched in, the fire department was shorthanded. The eighty or so firemen still in town could only fill companies to work seven or eight engines. In previous decades when there were too few firemen, the department could depend on a highly motivated populace to provide auxiliary crew at the scene of a fire. Unfortunately, regardless of enthusiasm, only 20 percent of the population remained in the city.[262]

In time, the influx of people, which included the British military and auxiliary personnel, Loyalists and their families moving back into the city and those who felt the city was safer than elsewhere, would provide able bodies to fill out the fire department. Just as important, the thousands moving in would provide more than enough people for the bucket brigades. But at this crucial moment, the half-sized fire department and the too-few inhabitants of New York were unprepared to fight large fires, especially those on the scale of the conflagration they were about to experience on the night of September 20.

Moreover, as every British report and Loyalist letter complained, there were no alarm bells. According to them, General Washington had ordered every bell in the city—church bells, fort bells, dock bells—removed and melted to be recast into cannons. This was, in the Loyalists' opinion, a heinous operation to deprive the city of its bells used for the alarm of fire.[263] Apparently, by that time, they did not feel wooden rattles were signal enough. On the other hand, a few moments after midnight on September 21, no one needed a bell or rattle to warn the city that it was on fire. For twenty miles in all directions, anyone could see across the horizon to the southern, blunt end of Manhattan, where sky and bay met the island, the city was burning.

The Great Fire Begins

Many witnesses pinpointed the origin of the fire, which began around midnight, to the neighborhood near Whitehall on the southern tip of Manhattan where Stuyvesant had built his 'Great White House' a century before.[264] No witness mentioned any suspicious activity. Some saw a few sailors socializing with women in a small, wooden house, a scene which more virtuous observers depicted as people of low moral standards drinking in a small, rude shed. The fire began, by these accounts, in a small building on the wharf near White Hall Slip (see the point labeled "1" on the map).

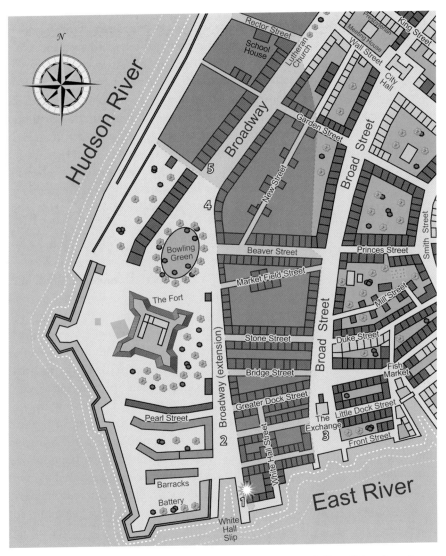

Above: The 1776 fire, from 12:00 to 2:00 a.m., began at White Hall (1) and blazed north with the wind. It was checked by the wide street to the west (2) and firefighters to the east (3). At 2:00 a.m. (4), 140 homes were destroyed, and the wind shifted (5).

Opposite: The FDNY, at the Exchange, stopped the initial blaze from crossing lower Broad Street (3). Although they were too undermanned to keep the fire from blazing north (4), they prevented it from going farther east.

Rapidly, the fire took hold and began to blaze north with the wind. Soon, the landmark Whitehall tavern, the "Fighting Cock," was blazing into the night sky and could be seen from a ship four miles away.[265]

The water of Whitehall Slip and the expanse of the Broadway extension ("2" on the map) provided a barrier to keep the flames from leaping west. The fort was not in danger. However, all the buildings on the blocks between the Broadway extension and Broad Street began to blaze into the night sky as a brisk wind carried the fire north. John Dash and other firemen who were still in the city positioned their engines in lower Broad Street. Even though they could make no headway against the wind-born flames going north, they were able to keep the flames from crossing Broad Street to the east. They saved the Exchange ("3" on the map), a large building with a market space below and a meeting hall above, even though it was in the middle of Broad Street, just a few yards from the roaring flames in the Whitehall blocks.

The Fire Spreads from White Hall to Beaver Street

Driven by the wind, the fire pushed up to and over Dock Street, then Bridge Street, Stone Street, Market Field and then to Beaver. At Beaver Street, under the best of conditions, the fire could have been stopped. Bowling Green provided a firebreak to the west, and the very broad Broad Street provided a firebreak to the east. With more engines in place, with lines of buckets filled with water and firemen with hooks and axes pulling down and playing water on the dozen or so buildings in the path of the fire, the fire might have been contained. But so many of the trained firemen who had the skills to form an effective firebreak were gone. Half of the engines were unmanned, and the bucket brigades were too few and too late. The fire burned over Beaver Street and kept going.

Even if every firefighting component in the city were at full force, the rate at which the fire was burning made it, with few exceptions, virtually unstoppable. In its first two hours, it destroyed over a dozen buildings every ten minutes. Around 2:00 a.m., after the fire had crossed over Beaver Street and burned six buildings on the east side of Broadway ("4" on the map), the wind changed direction from the north to the northwest. This caused the fire to take a dogleg left to the northwest and cross Broadway. The west side of Broadway began to burn ("5" on the map).

AFTER 2:00 A.M., WEST OF BROADWAY BURNS

That was bad for the area west of Broadway but good for the rest of the city to its east. Once the fire crossed Broadway, it burned to the Hudson River to the west while its eastern edge went up New Street. The firefighting efforts of British sailors and soldiers who were then on the ground, helping the engine teams, along with the change in wind, affected a small miracle that spared the buildings on Broad Street north of Beaver Street.

Still driven by the wind that was blowing to the north and west, the fire went through the intersection of New and Garden Streets, leaving the houses on New Street above Garden Street untouched. It was as if the fire demon wanted to get to Trinity Church, a Loyalist-dominated parish, as directly as possible, and it could not be bothered with the "little" buildings on the east side of Broadway any longer.

Several witnesses, however, would later say that the fire demon had help. "A few minutes after the fire was discovered at White Hall, it was observed to break out in five or six other places, at a considerable distance." The question was whether a mass of sparks and flaming flakes caused these secondary fires or if they were caused by deliberate arson. In either case, many witnesses saw buildings to the north and west of the leading body of the fire burning long before the main blaze had crossed Broadway—in fact, even before it had crossed Stone Street.

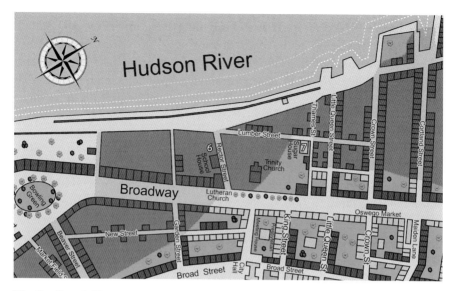

The fire, from 2:00 to 4:00 a.m., spread up Broadway, west to the Hudson and then north. It then burned to the schoolhouse (6) and the Lutheran and Trinity Churches. Narrowed, the fire crossed Thames Street at the Sugar House (7).

THE FIRE BURNS TOWARD TRINITY CHURCH

Once again, the firefighters were able to stop the fire from going north, aided by the strong wind blowing the flames and sparks away from Garden Street toward Broadway. As it happened, the buildings on New Street, above Garden Street, and all but five on the east side of Broadway were spared. The fire never reached Wall Street. Once it went over Broadway, it burned up its west side. The fire, then on both sides of Broadway, seemed to converge on Rector Street at the Lutheran church and the schoolhouse just south of Trinity Church.

The Lutheran church and the schoolhouse ("6" on the map) were the next prominent buildings to catch fire from what seemed to be an unstoppable wave of flames. Then came Trinity Church, one of the largest and most exquisite buildings in the city. It was an Anglican church with a congregation that was strongly Loyalist and a clergy who had long opposed the Revolutionary movement in sermons and print.[266] As reported, "The steeple, which was 140 feet high, the upper part wood…resembled a vast pyramid of fire, exhibiting a most grand and awful spectacle."[267]

It was from the fires west of Broadway, particularly the fire at Trinity Church itself, that initiated the allegations of conspiracy and arson. Several witnesses (see link to sworn testimonies) saw fires west of Broadway before the wave of flame roared over Beaver Street.[268] Other witnesses saw wind-born, blazing flakes ignite small flames on Trinity Church in the first hour of the fire before the Lutheran church was burning.

Later, several witnesses saw flakes and sparks from the Lutheran church finally catch Trinity Church's steeple on fire and engulf it in flames.[269] It seems that an hour or so before the steeple was set on fire from the Lutheran church's blaze, Trinity Church had been under assault and burning from small, flaming projectiles launched by blazes farther south of Rector Street. On this night in September 1776, once the out-of-control forces of nature exploded into a firestorm, Trinity Church did not need any human agency to burn it down. Even though a well-intentioned arsonist might have applied, it was already doomed.

The firestorm destroyed Trinity Church. Its 140-foot-tall wooden steeple gathered and encouraged fiery flakes that would have challenged the effective reach of the fire engines, even if they were on the ground at the time, which they were not. The fire had traveled so far so fast that Dash, Alstine and other leaders had not been able to disengage from the fire east of Broadway soon enough to save the church, the rector's house and other church property on Lumber Street, a block west of Broadway.

The delay in their redeployment had another crucial consequence: they lost the opportunity to stop the fire at the northwest corner of the Trinity block at Lumber and Thames Streets. The area north of the church had a few trees, but they would not feed the wall of flames as the closely spaced buildings to the south did. Moreover, the one prominent building near that corner, Van Courtlandt's Sugar House ("7" on the map), proved to be remarkably, if not miraculously, fire-resistant. The open space and the sugar house squeezed the path of the fire into a narrow front as it came into Thames Street—perhaps 100 to 150 feet wide, much more manageable than the football fields of flames to the south. But the firefighting force, stretched as thin as it was, could not, at the time, extend all the way to the Hudson River. The fire crossed north over Thames Street and fanned back east.

Of course, this narrowed front was an opportunity to obstruct the fire only if the fire were moving north under its own energy. If arsonists supplemented the fire north of the Trinity block, they would have severely undermined the ability of the firefighters to arrest the flames. The forensic evidence for arson would eventually include bundles of incendiary firesticks in shops and warehouses and under the coats of people walking up and

VAN CORTLANDT'S SUGAR-HOUSE.

The Sugar House, located just a block north of Trinity Church, did not burn, narrowed the blaze and provided an opportunity for a firebreak.

down Broadway. It would also include barrels of fused gunpowder inside buildings—one close enough to endanger St. Paul's Church.

There was also the suspiciously circumstantial path of the fire. Once over Thames Street, it reversed direction and headed east on a broad front. What caused it to come back to the east again, into a wind that was presumably still blowing northwest? Did the wind change direction? The firefighters did not select the natural, human or demonic forces manipulating the fire that night, they took their small segment of hell on earth where they found it and moved their engines north on Broadway.

Somebody Fought This Fire

The FDNY redeployment saved much of the west side of Broadway—no building bordering the street was burned north of the Trinity block. That included the prominent structures such as the Oswego Market ("8" on the map) and St. Paul's Church ("9" on the map). The footprint of the fire on the map shows what a close-run operation it had been. The fire was traveling north at a rate of about a block an hour. Assuming it traveled east at a similar rate, the fire would have reached Broadway at Thames Street around daylight, but it never got that far; it was stopped a block short. It would have reached Oswego Market in the early morning, but it was stopped there, too, five houses from Broadway. As Ron Coleman, a California fire chief and former president of the International Association

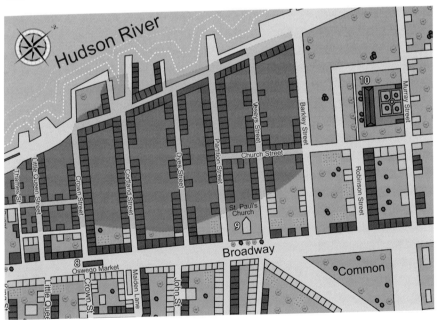

The fire, after 4:00 a.m., burned north and east until it was stopped by firemen before it reached Broadway, saving the Oswego Market (8) and St. Paul's Church (9). The fire was finally quenched at the yard of King's College (10).

The FDNY, at St. Paul's, saved not only the church but also the entire west side of Broadway north of Trinity. As before British soldiers proved crucial to the firefighting effort.

The fire ends at Kings College.

of Fire Chiefs, has observed: "When you look at a footprint of a fire, where there are distinct boundaries the fire did not cross—that is no accident; somebody fought that fire."[270]

It is likely that Dash and his engines provided the crucial intervention to stop the fire from getting back to Broadway. British soldiers and sailors, having served their apprenticeships in firefighting for the previous six hours, had also developed effective techniques to create firebreaks. The fire reached a few buildings at the corner of Dyes Street and Broadway, but that was as far east as the fire got after 4:00 a.m. If Dash and his company had not been successful, St. Paul's would have been assaulted by flames from both the south and west, making its defense more difficult, if not impossible.

As firefighters pushed the fire back to Church Street, the front of the fire narrowed once again, and on reaching the open ground in front of King's College ("10" on the map), it lost its fuel. There were still sparks flying until about 11:00 a.m., but by that time, a corps of British soldiers, sailors, townspeople and students, along with the firemen, were able to control the blaze and stop it at Barkley Street.

AFTERMATH OF THE FIRE

Firefighting efforts, uncoordinated and short-handed at first, did manage to save most of the city, although that must have seemed small comfort to the thousands who had lost their homes, schools, churches, shops, warehouses and factories. Trinity Church experienced the most substantial loss. The church burned that night, together with its rector's house and two hundred houses that stood on the church's property, which amounted to 40 percent of the buildings destroyed. Trinity's rector, Charles Inglis, estimated the loss to the church at £25,000 sterling or about $5 million in America's twenty-first-century currency, not counting the loss in rental revenue. As Trinity was a center of the Loyalists' religious and social community, it may have been more than an accident that fire engulfed this area of the west side. Inglis certainly thought so: "The church corporation suffered prodigiously, as was evidently intended."[271]

From their northern Manhattan encampments, Washington and his army watched with morbid fascination as the conflagration burned the town. Washington's feeling then was, "Providence, or some good honest fellow, has done more for us than we were disposed to do for ourselves."[272] A typical Patriot sentiment reinforced his commander's: "Had not the wind, as it

Trinity Church before the fire extended 148 feet, from its tower facing the Hudson River to its chancel on Broadway near Wall Street. Its 175-foot-tall spire could be seen as far away as New Jersey and Long Island.

veered to the west died away, the remainder of that nest of vipers would have been destroyed."[273] If Patriot sentiments, thus expressed, were in fact translated into action, there would be little speculation as to the political affiliation of those who might have aided and abetted the fire that night. In fact, some who believe Patriots set the fires, criticize them for not doing it more effectively.

The devastation had little effect on the British build-up or their execution of the war. Their troops barracked in virtually every church and large public building in the city and in the houses and shops vacated by the Patriots. The troops with their families, however, along with the five hundred buildings destroyed, did reduce the remaining housing stock available for the tens of thousands who were streaming back into town over the next few years.[274]

Trinity Church after the fire left it in ruins, with only the shell of its walls and its fragmented tower still standing. To the south, across Rector Street, the hollowed-out remnants of the Lutheran Church can be seen.

It was a formula for suffering—a burned-out town; a military occupation with families, servants and concubines; thousands of destitute refugees; and enough food and shelter for only the troops and those who could afford it. Tents massed among the ruins soon exuded a stench remarkable even to the British who were familiar with London slums.[275] With minimal sanitation and a meager diet, the health of those in the slum tents was poor. Disease and malnutrition increased mortality. Except for the sight and smells of the slum, the British war effort was unaffected.

WHO DID IT? NO CREDIBLE EVIDENCE OF ARSON VS. PATRIOTS BURNED THEIR OWN TOWN

The first answer (no credible evidence) assumes that the fire was caused accidentally and then was propagated by an overwhelming firestorm. A stiff wind and the energy of the conflagration itself projected fiery flakes and sparks hundreds of yards in advance of the main wall of flames, traveling north at first and then northwest. With 80 percent of the general population and over half the fire department gone, efforts to contain the blaze were compromised. Those who were arrested the night of the fire were just hapless civilians—some trying to fight the fire—who were pounced on by British soldiers who were overly suspicious of anyone not in a British uniform. According to this narrative, the fire was finally stopped by firemen, civilians and students (no British troops in this version) just before it reached King's College, about one mile from its origin.

This was a story congenial to and propagated by the continental congress that was then in Philadelphia, the New York proto-state government and other leaders of the Revolution. Early historians did their part with a good spin on the events of September 20. One even removed the record of witnesses who saw arsonists and vandals from the otherwise comprehensive and definitive *American Archives*.[276]

Some variations of this story had British troops burning the city, but the irrationality of the British destroying their own secure and comfortable accommodations just before winter set in made no sense to anyone but a Patriot zealot. Moreover, if the British wanted to destroy the city, they could have easily done it months before with only the large warships then in the harbor. British commanders could also point to their scrupulous and comprehensive placement of guards throughout the city to maintain order and prevent looting as their troops moved in.[277]

The second view (Patriots burned their own town) is like the first one when relating the origin, progress and extent of the main blaze. The crucial differences in this version were the reports of the eruption of secondary fires soon after the main blaze. These reports judged these fires to be too distant from the original fire for airborne sparks or flaming flakes to ignite them. This narrative concluded that the cause of these secondary fires was arson— that is, they had been deliberately set.

A little over a week after the fire, Hugh Gaine's Loyalist newspaper published an early and definitive version of this narrative. From the *New-York Gazette*:

> *On Saturday the 21ˢᵗ Instant, we had a terrible fire in this city, which consumed about one thousand houses, or nearly a fourth of the whole city.[278]…The rebel army having carried off all the bells of the city, the alarm could not be speedily communicated; and very few of the citizens*

were in town, most of them being driven out by the calamities of war.…A few minutes after the fire was discovered at White-Hall, it was observed to break out in five or six other Places, at a considerable distance.…

The officers of the army and navy, the seamen and soldiers, greatly exerted themselves.…To their vigorous efforts…it is owing, under providence, that the whole city was not consumed; for the number of inhabitants was small, the pumps and fire engines were much out of order…together with the removal of our bells, the time and place of the fire's breaking out, when the wind was south, the city's being set on fire in so many places at nearly the same time, so many incendiaries being caught in the very fact of setting fire to houses…clearly evince beyond the possibility of doubt, that this diabolical affair was the result of a preconcerted, deliberate scheme.[279]

Historians have continued the controversy over these two opposing narratives. The differences of opinion are alive, even into the twenty-first century. The "no credible evidence" camp includes several well-known Pulitzer Prize winners. More recently, historian Benjamin Carp has introduced convincing evidence in his article "The Night the Yankees Burned Broadway." His extensive analysis concludes: "Though we cannot ascribe specific responsibility, we can assert in the broadest terms that Americans sympathetic to the Whig cause [i.e., Patriots] set New York City on fire in September 1776."[280]

Among the new sources of evidence Carp introduced was the Carleton Commission, a formal British investigation into the cause of and culpability for the fire. Its sworn testimonies of forty witnesses to the fire is persuasive. Since the commission's report definitively ascribes culpability for the fire, if accepted as accurately reflecting the reality of the 1776 New York fire, it is described in more detail in the next chapter.

THE CARLETON COMMISSION

A Commission Formed to Investigate the Fire

Gaine's newspaper account, published in the *New-York Gazette* for Loyalist consumption, included the facts of the fire as understood by the British and the Loyalists who were still in the city at the time of the fire in 1776. In October 1783, at the end of the war, General Guy Carleton, the commander in chief of the British forces in North America, directed a commission to investigate the disastrous New York fire of 1776. He wanted a comprehensive report focused on whether the fire was accidental, deliberate but uncoordinated or planned and coordinated, "the effect of design." If by design, the commission was to determine what higher authority directed the arsonists.[281]

While the commissioners were to perform the task "with all convenient speed," the emphasis was on speed, not convenience. It was the last months of 1783, and the commissioners could not dawdle. Tens of thousands of British troops and auxiliaries, Loyalists, freed people, rich merchants and others who felt threatened by the incipient Revolutionary regime were sailing away as fast as they could. The commissioners themselves, as British officers, would be boarding ships in less than six weeks. Many of their witnesses would also be on those ships, sailing into their uncertain futures.

There were "diverse, important considerations" for the Commissioners to make a credible determination of the cause and culpability for the fire. Not the least of these considerations were the "gray areas" of the peace treaty negotiated in Paris, formally ending the Revolutionary War. The treaty specified property rights and compensation but still contained seeds of controversy. George Washington had protested Carleton's policy permitting the enslaved to flee the country as "a departure both from the letter and spirit" of the treaty. Carleton countered that these former enslaved people had been previously freed by a pact with the British government. As such, they were no longer "property of American inhabitants" and thus not covered by the treaty as it stood. The question of compensation, if any, had to be decided by future negotiations. Thus, Carleton maintained the freedom of the formerly enslaved, despite Washington's best efforts to uphold the property rights of their former owners.[282]

Carleton also anticipated that both Loyalist and Patriot New York property owners would seek compensation for their buildings that had been destroyed in the fire. The question was "compensation from whom." Carleton apparently felt it was his duty to have as much factual evidence as possible to limit the liability of the British government for the 1776 fire. To restrict potential claims, his commission was looking for evidence of what the British already believed: the King's troops did nothing but try to save the city, and many Americans, with or without orders and acting in concert or by themselves, started fires to burn their own city. The commission thus sought proof "beyond the possibility of doubt" of American culpability as reported six years before.

Carleton appointed three senior British officers to the commission, a brigadier general and two majors. Ward Chipman, a civilian Loyalist lawyer and member of an earlier commission for claims against the British army, served as the recorder for the commission.[283] Chipman transcribed thirty-nine testimonies over the next three weeks that yielded about one hundred written manuscript pages.

Each witness, called individually before the panel of commissioners, would make a short statement of their experience and observations at the fire and answer eight or nine questions. The questions did not vary much from witness to witness. Did the witness ever suppose the fire was accidental—set by the king's troops designedly or otherwise? Were the pumps and fire buckets vandalized? Did they see anyone set fires or obstruct those fighting it? What did they know of how the fire(s) started? What direction was the wind? Appointed on October 18, 1783, the commission met and took its first deposition two days later.[284]

Nearly three-quarters of the witnesses were British military members, auxiliaries and Loyalist civilians. They held strong pro-British sympathies, and most of them would be on the boats, leaving the city, within weeks. Assuming their views of the fire coincided with the *Mercury Gazette*'s in 1776, it seemed quite likely that the commission would get from them the "proof" of British innocence and Patriot culpability they expected.

The remaining witnesses were either Patriots or less-politically-active Loyalists, like the firemen who intended to stay in the city after the British evacuation. Collectively, those who were staying had little reason to give a pro-British "spin" to their accounts of the conflagration. It is therefore surprising that the depositions by the witnesses from both groups, with few exceptions, proved remarkably consistent and mutually reinforcing. It is even more surprising that evidence from accredited American sources, such as letters from Washington, would corroborate several key testimonies.

Many Fires Set or Just Wind-Blown Sparks?

John Dash, a tinsmith and veteran fireman, was essentially the commission's first "expert" witness. His occupation in working metals enabled him to maintain and repair fire engines in the prewar department. Appointed by the British to manage the engines in 1776, he with four other Loyalists who directed the firefighting efforts of the department during the Revolution. Dash testified that based on his long experience, he did not "believe it possible that the fire could have communicated to different parts of the city…but verily believes that it was purposely set on fire in different places, that he never supposed the fire accidental." He remembered that as soon as he was on the ground at White Hall, moments after the first alarm, he found that a fire had burned a half a mile away, behind Trinity Church, near the Hudson River.[285]

Dash, at the time, had little incentive to put a pro-British slant on his testimony. As with the other department leaders, he intended to stay in New York after the British evacuation. In just five weeks, the British were gone. In late November 1776, while a new city government was being formed, the New York state government managed the affairs of the city. Dash and the four other Loyalist leaders proposed a plan directly to New York's governor, George Clinton, to organize the postwar fire department.[286] For a Loyalist lobbying to supervise the postwar fire department and presumably wanting to ingratiate himself with the new Patriot government, his testimony appeared quite candid and far from self-serving.

Like Dash, about half of those testifying saw multiple fires far from the original blaze and concluded they could only be acts of deliberate arson.

Several of those witnesses were on ships in the harbor with a "front-row," panoramic view of the progress of the fire. Of course, to meet standards of proof for many Americans, there would need to be an objective, unimpeachable eyewitness unconnected with the British commission, an American war hero would be a plus. Meet John Joseph Henry.

Henry was an American veteran of the Revolution and was later the president of the Second Judicial District in Pennsylvania. He had enlisted in the Pennsylvania militia at sixteen and marched with Benedict Arnold to the ill-fated attack on Quebec early in the war, where he was taken prisoner. As a result of his imprisonment and for the rest of his life, he suffered from the effects of scurvy. Still, he persevered after the war, in chronic poor health, to get a law degree, practice law and, later, was appointed to head the Second Judicial District.[287] Henry wrote a book describing the Canadian campaign and his subsequent captivity by the British. It was from a British prison ship in New York Harbor that he witnessed the fire.

> *Laying directly south of the city and in a range with Broadway, we had a fair and full view of the whole process. The persons in the ships nearer to the town than we were uniformly held the same opinion....My own view of the distant beginnings of the fire in various spots, remote from each other, and the manner of its spreading, impressed my mind with the belief, that the burning of the city was the doings of the most low and vile persons...*[288]
>
> *It was not until some years afterwards that a doubt was created...an ascription was made, of the firing of the city, to accidental circumstances.... It may be well that a nation, in the heat and turbulence of war, should endeavor to promote its interests by propagating reports of its own innocence and prowess and accusing its enemy of flagrant enormity and dastardliness, (as was done in this particular case,) but when peace comes, let us, in God's name, do justice to them and to ourselves...as the fact occurred within my own view, the eloquence of Cicero could not convince me that the firing was accidental.*[289]

The observations of the fire in its early stage from Dash, Henry and others tilt reasonable opinion toward the hypothesis of multiple arsons. In later stages of the fire, with flaming flakes and sparks being launched for hundreds of yards, it would be difficult to assign the proximate cause of any given blaze. Many buildings, Trinity Church, for example, ignited at different stages of the fire from sparks far away and then later from the Lutheran church across Rector Street nearby. But the many testimonies describing multiple fires before the small, original blaze gathered momentum, assuming they are accurate, strongly suggest multiple fires were deliberately set. Of course, if so many fires were deliberately being set, where were the arsonists? Snaring an arsonist or two "red-handed" would add to the convincing evidence of deliberate arson.

CAUGHT IN THE ACT

The cool, windy September midnight in Manhattan was darker than normal because not all of the lamps had been replaced since the British army had regained control of the city. John Grundy, a private in His Majesty's Forty-Third Regiment of Foot, was on guard duty at city hall when he saw the flickering glimmer at the other end of Broad Street, near the Exchange. By the time Grundy was later relieved from guard duty, the glimmer from a small shed had become a blaze of several blocks from Broad Street west to the fort. He was ordered into that part of the city to find the arsonists—if there were any—and stop them.

Heading in the direction of the Exchange, he heard a cry: "Soldiers, soldiers, there is a man setting fire to the town!" Rushing through lower Broad Street, he saw a man holding a burning torch against the roof of a shed. Grundy knocked the torch out of his hand but was unable to subdue him. The man fled down Little Dock Street toward the Fly Market. Grundy caught up with him at a dock on the East River as he attempted to escape by boat. According to bystanders, he had offered two dollars for an oar. Grundy forcibly arrested the man and remanded him to the Provost, the detention camp and prison set up by the British military for both civilian and military offenders.[290]

Grundy returned to the Provost later to confirm that his detainee's arrest was for arson. The prisoner was Amos Fellows, a captain in Colonel Samuel Chapman's Twenty-Second Connecticut militia regiment. Being an American officer caught on the ground during the fire did not bode well for him.[291] The British released most of the approximately two hundred suspects who had been arrested during the fire, but they did not extend this leniency to American officers.

Once imprisoned, the officers could only hope for parole or exchange before they died in prison, which many did. Historian Edwin Burroughs estimated that more American soldiers died in British prisons, fifteen to eighteen thousand, than were killed in combat during the war.[292] There is little doubt that the British believed Fellows guilty as accused. He was reported to be "treated with uncommon severity, whereby his life is in danger."[293] In spite of the direct efforts of George Washington to secure his early release, Fellows died in prison in early 1777.[294]

The letters of George Washington himself, attempting to save Fellows, corroborates Grundy's testimony before the commission. The Grundy testimony was unique. Other testimonies give plausible circumstantial evidence of arson but do not claim to have witnessed an arsonist in the act of torching a building.

For example, George Kerr, another private in the Forty-Third Regiment, patrolled on the west side of Broadway near St. Paul's Church, the focus of the firefighting efforts by the fire department, soldiers and civilians after 4:00 a.m. He, with a few backup soldiers, entered a house behind St. Paul's, where five men and a woman were assembled in a small room where they had put a keg of gunpowder encased in bundles of firesticks. There was a small fire heating the room, and candles illuminated it.

Although the woman offered Kerr money to let them go, he and his team corralled the men and the barrel of gunpowder and turned them in to the Provost.[295] Perhaps he let the woman go. There was no further mention of money. Those who were arrested claimed they often met with a barrel or two of gunpowder in the small room behind St. Paul's, even before the war. Admittedly, this evidence is circumstantial, since none of the arrestees were putting a candle to the fuse. But they were less than thirty or forty yards from a blazing conflagration. If it was that important for them to meet in the path of a firestorm, it would have been marginally safer to not bring the explosives to their "regular" meeting just that once. It would also have been safer for the neighborhood, since the explosives were powerful enough to blow a big hole in a big church.

FIRESTICKS: HOW SO MANY FIRES COULD START SO FAST

Testimony from another soldier, John Cochran, reinforced what the commission had heard from many witnesses—there were widespread stocks of combustible firesticks on or near the fireground. Cochran, along with some other soldiers, seized yet another suspect as he walked up Broadway toward the head of the fire. He made no effort to hide the combustibles under his brown coat. Cochran could easily see the "bunch of matches" under his arm because these matches were not small toothpick-size slivers of wood but thick wooden sticks that were eighteen inches long. The suspect, perhaps feeling the soldiers would be indifferent to his story that he was removing the firesticks from houses to protect them from fire, tried to escape. Cochran and his companions caught him and took him to the Provost Detention Camp.[296]

As the inquiry continued, the commissioners gradually uncovered the source of the firesticks. The Patriot military had manufactured large numbers of the firesticks, often referred to as "matches," for use as components of a fireship or fire raft. The firesticks were eighteen inches long, one inch square of white cedar or walnut, with six inches of flammable rosin and brimstone (sulfurous compounds) saturating one or both ends.[297] The shipbuilders would pack bundles of thirty to fifty firesticks around barrels of gunpowder on an expendable fireship, such as a small harbor boat or a purpose-built raft. Volunteer sailors would attempt to steer the ship as close as possible to an enemy warship, using the wind, current and tide. They then would ignite the fuse for the floating combustible mass, which would soon explode into smithereens of flame hopefully close enough to the warship to set it on fire.

For the sailors, this was a hazardous, almost suicidal, duty. They had to escape in a small boat at exactly the right moment after the fireship was in flames but before the explosion. Of course, even before they were close to any warship, they might have to evade cannons firing both grapeshot and solid shot at their relatively small vessel. In addition, there might be one hundred or more marine sharpshooters on the deck of the warship firing at them as soon as they came into range from a few hundred yards out. On the open sea, where warships could maneuver, fireships proved virtually useless. With ships at anchor in a harbor and crews ashore, they could be devastating.[298]

Washington may not have known the sizable effort in New York to produce combustibles for fireships. However, he did know that Captain Hazelwood, an experienced fireship builder from Philadelphia, had been in New York for some time and built and armed several fire vessels, which Washington called in to support Fort Washington.[299] He also, no doubt, knew the results of fireships used against the British ship *Phoenix* in the East River. Although the *Phoenix* escaped, one of its support vessels was burned to the water and yielded "one iron six-pounder, two three-pounders, one two-pounder, ten swivels, a caboose, some gunbarrels, cutlasses, grapplings, chains, &c."[300] It was not exactly a big win, but any positive news in August 1776 was welcome.

Many of the two hundred suspects taken to the Provost, the detention center, were arrested for possessing firesticks. The common alibi of those

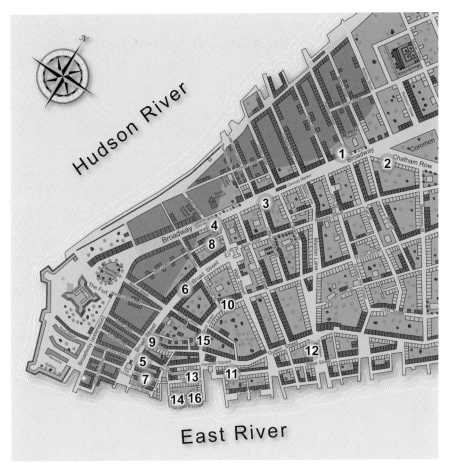

Combustible explosives, bundles of eighteen-inch-long firesticks and kegs of fused gunpowder, were discovered on potential arsonists and in buildings during and just after the fire, suggesting the blaze was more than just an accident.

arrested with firesticks was that they were removing them from their homes and businesses as a safety measure. This, of course, begged the question of why the firesticks were so widely distributed in the first place. After the fire, General Robertson, the British commander for New York, deputized several teams to search for stocks of combustibles and remove them. They found a surprising number of firestick bundles and even a few fused barrels of gunpowder. Robertson's searches demonstrated how widely distributed the combustibles had been. If some people were trying to burn down the town, they had industrial quantities of firesticks to do it. In some ways, New York was lucky to lose only 20 percent or so of its buildings.

of Witnesses Who Testified

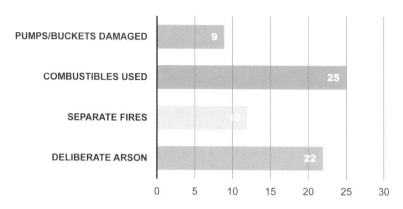

The 1783 Carleton Commission took the sworn testimony of eyewitnesses who saw fire equipment damaged, combustibles, fires erupting far from the original blaze and an arsonist torching sheds.

Cruger's Wharf was the center for storing the firesticks and assembling the firebomb ships in New York.[301] Witnesses had seen large bundles of firesticks in its warehouses and in the nearby workshops. Even after the fire, several men and women, just before they were arrested, pilfered the matches for their own hearths, a small profit or Revolutionary mayhem.[302]

The search discovered bundles of firesticks, which survived, intact, east of the path of the fire. Assuming firesticks had been planted as widely to the west of Broad Street as they were to its east, there can be little doubt that their explosions expanded and accelerated the fire as it flamed north. They may have been the largest component of the deliberate arson that night.

In summary, a dozen witnesses testified that they saw blazes far from the original fire, which they believed were deliberately set, not caused by the sparks. Other witnesses described their direct experiences with exploding chimneys, arsonists torching sheds and fleeing burning buildings and groups inexplicably in the path of the firestorm with fused barrels of gunpowder. Several anecdotal testimonies reinforced the firsthand accounts. And then there were the firesticks, which provided the easy means of starting or accelerating the fire. If these testimonies accurately reflect the reality of the great fire, it is reasonable to conclude that they provide credible evidence of deliberate arson, even to twenty-first-century Americans, let alone to an eighteenth-century British military commission that had already moved on to its next agenda item.

PLANNED AND COORDINATED?

As the British found convincing evidence that the fire was deliberately set in several places, their continuing inquiries focused on whether the fires were planned or coordinated. Hard evidence of coordination from their point of view would be the discovery of American army officers in New York during and after the fire. What purpose would the American officers have behind enemy lines if not to coordinate disruption? And what better disruption than a large fire?

The British released most of the approximately two hundred suspects arrested during the fire. Sometimes, the evidence was weak or contradictory, but many were released when, just a few days before, they were hiding matches under their coats while walking near the fire. For whatever reasons, General Howe did not feel it worth the effort to prosecute or imprison them. Perhaps he wanted his army to focus on the destruction of Washington's army and felt that a major inquiry would be an unnecessary diversion. However, captured American officers did not receive any reprieves and had no trials, just harsh imprisonment. The commission wanted to know what their orders were, if any.

Among the notable American officers caught in New York was Abraham Van Dyke, a New York native and captain of the city's Grenadier Company. The Grenadier Company, "a long-established militia unit in the city," was an elite company with members who were sometimes physically larger and usually better trained, more experienced and more highly motivated than those in other militia units. Van Dyke himself had served as a marine lieutenant in the French and Indian War. His company had earned high praise in the spring of 1776 for its solid and efficient construction of a circular battery northwest of the city on the Hudson River.[303]

When General Israel Putnam finally moved the last American troops out of Manhattan, they just barely slipped by a large force of British pushing west to cut them off. Virtually the entire army managed this timely escape. Unfortunately, Van Dyke, the last to join the retreat, was not among them. Facing certain capture if he attempted to dodge through the British lines, he returned to the city and was safely taken into the house of a friend called Leary. The "young lady" of the house attempted to inform his American commander of his location, but the British, by that time, had blocked communications north out of the city.[304]

According to Van Dyke, he was still in the house when the fire erupted. He did not venture out of the house, as it was dangerous for anyone not in a British uniform to walk the streets.[305] Even so, he might have escaped the notice of the British altogether had a disaffected servant or neighbor not directed British lieutenant Innes with a small squad to the house, where Van Dyke hid. Even then, his "young lady" guardian misdirected Innes, who searched the whole house before he finally found Van Dyke "secreted in a closet of one of the bed chambers."[306]

Van Dyke, fifty-eight years old at the time of his capture, was perhaps a little older than what the British ideally would have typecast as their American firebrand. However, as an experienced American officer, he could certainly have coordinated the arson, which the British presumed for his continued incarceration. Captain Van Dyke was more fortunate than Fellows, the captain from Connecticut who Washington tried to save. He would survive his incarceration and be exchanged in 1778, almost two years later.[307]

There were many American officers in New York at the time of the fire. Some, like Van Dyke, had been trapped when the bulk of the American force evacuated north to Harlem. Others, like Fellows, had gone underground to take the fight directly to the enemy. Others who were in New York as prisoners from the battles on Long Island might have gained freedom in the confusion of the fire or, conceivably, might already have been paroled.[308] Other officers, like Captain Nathan Hale of Knowlton's Rangers, were in the city on "business," which, in his case, was to gather intelligence about British positions. It is possible that Hale helped to burn the city before he was arrested and executed.[309] However, it is much more likely that after collecting the valuable information for which he was sent, he was seeking an unnoticed exit back to American lines.[310]

There were several other less-celebrated American officers who reportedly died during the fire or were arrested. The *New-York Gazette* told of another captain, this one in the Continental army from New England, who was rescued from an angry mob by the British general Robertson.[311] In addition to matches, he had £500 on him, which was deemed to be as incriminating as the combustibles. In two other incidents, Richard Brown, a second lieutenant in a Pennsylvania rifle regiment, and William Smith, an officer in a New England regiment, were taken with matches in their hands "and sacrificed on the spot to the fury of the soldiers."[312]

However, the actions of several individual officers did not come close to proving a coordinated effort by Washington or even an ambitious regimental commander to burn the city. Even the testimonies garnered by the commission, at their anecdotal best, could only implicate a lieutenant colonel. Even more convincing of the absence of a plan or coordination at the highest level were three American Patriots who volunteered to testify.

The Testimony of American Patriots

Comfort Sands had been a New York provincial (soon to be state) legislator in 1776. He became the first auditor general for the State of New York, a position he held until 1782.[313] Sands assured the commission that the fire was not ordered by any American authority, civil or military leader, and as far as he knew, it was not even debated in congress. Although he was not in the city at the time, Sands believed the fire to be "largely accidental." As a property owner, he could not comprehend why any American would want to burn the city in the first place.

Isaac Stoutenburgh was a gunsmith like his father, Isaac, and his uncle Jacobus, the fire chief. He was also a fireman and became one of Jacobus's assistants. At the beginning of the war, he formed a company of militia in the city and eventually became a lieutenant colonel. He also served as a provincial and state legislator for most of the war. In separate testimony, Isaac Stoutenburgh reinforced Sands's testimony that no one in authority ordered the fire to be set.

Isaac Stoutenburgh was a fireman and gunsmith. A lieutenant colonel in the militia company he formed, he also served as a state senator. After the war, as an Alderman, he helped rebuild the city.

The commission had speculated that so many had abandoned the city because they had advanced knowledge of the fire plot. Stoutenburgh responded that the populace fled not from any plot, real or imagined, but from the fear of bombardment and the "general calamities of war." Far from wanting the city to burn, he asserted that American authorities had collected the fire buckets from abandoned houses and secured them in city hall, where they would be readily available in the case of an emergency.[314]

In addition to the two New York legislators, there was another witness who was pro-American, that is, a Patriot, William Ellsworth. Ellsworth was a fireman before the war and fought with the American military during the war. He testified that congress had directed him and others to collect buckets from abandoned houses in the summer of 1776. This, of course, reinforced Stoutenburgh's testimony. Ellsworth added the compelling details of how difficult it had been to get the buckets. They had to pick locks to get through secured doors, and even then, the buckets were often hidden.[315] Ellsworth, testifying independently, did not have Comfort Sands's rather naive view that no Americans would favor burning the city before the British occupation. "Several individuals said they would sooner set fire to their own houses than leave them for the use of British troops."[316]

CONCLUSIONS

Although Ward Chipman's final report in London might have included the commission's relevant conclusions, the "findings" of the commission are not explicitly included in the pages of the manuscript at the New-York Historical Society. However, if the commission accepted the testimonies to accurately represent the reality of September 21, 1776, it would most likely have come to the following conclusions:

- The fires were not accidental, although the initial blaze might have been.
- Fires far from the initial fire were set within the first hour.
- Hidden combustibles were found on people and in caches throughout the city.
- The king's troops stopped arsonists from burning more of the city.
- Patriots were caught in the act of setting fires; some were killed, and many were arrested.

- City water pumps and fire buckets were vandalized.
- There was no high-level congress or American military order to burn the city.

If the testimonies reflect what happened in the fire of 1776, it is reasonable to conclude that at least some of the destruction was the result of deliberate arson. Although the original fire might have been accidental, the fact that several fires occurred within an hour so far from that initial blaze could persuade us, as it did many original witnesses, that the conflagration was more than mere chance or an unfortunate mistake.

FDNY DURING THE REVOLUTION (1777–83)

*T*he fire department had been unprepared for the fire of 1776. In September, it was organized to the extent that there were still several foremen, usually Loyalists, in command of individual engines. The fire companies themselves were shorthanded, with perhaps only half of the early 1776 department remaining in town. Even with British sailors and soldiers filling in some of the ranks of the bucket brigades, the skilled teams that could form effective firebreaks were absent during the blaze, which squandered opportunities to contain the fire before it crossed Broadway and, later, to the area north of Trinity Church. Of course, firefighters had little help from the arsonists, who continued to set buildings on fire or the vandals who disabled the well pumps and cut up fire buckets.

However, even with those drawbacks, there is clear evidence that the FDNY did fight the fire. At the fire's origin, near White Hall Slip in the middle of Broad Street, stood the Exchange, a large, covered market with a second-story meeting hall. Even though it was just a few yards from the raging blaze, the Exchange marvelously survived, intact. The agent for that marvel was fireman John Dash, who placed the first engines on the ground so that they were able to block the inferno to the east.

Later that night, Dash and several foremen moved the engines from White Hall north on Broadway, toward the Oswego Market and St. Paul's. The blaze that had swept to the Hudson River was headed back toward Broadway. Near St. Paul's, between Courtland and Dyes Street, a house or two from Broadway, the FDNY stopped the fire. Had it reached Broadway, St. Paul's might have suffered damage as severe as that suffered by Trinity Church. It was again the FDNY that was the primary force blocking the blaze from destroying buildings on Broadway itself north of Trinity Church.[317]

Not all New York firemen in 1776 were fighting fires in September. At least a third had joined the Patriot military to resist the British invasion. Many, although not in the military, worked as auxiliaries to keep Washington's army in the field, such as Jacobus Stoutenburgh's most likely role as gunsmith. Others, like Stoutenburgh's nephew Isaac, formerly his assistant engineer, had volunteered for city and county militias as early as 1775. Many firemen also joined the "national" Continental army, authorized by the continental congress and soon commanded by Washington.[318]

Isaac continued to participate in the Patriot mobilization by consolidating the city militia company he had raised with three other companies to form a battalion. They then asked congress to appoint a slate of officers, a colonel, a lieutenant colonel and a major, congenial to the several companies. As that battalion grew into a regiment, Isaac was promoted to major, and by the middle of 1776, he was commissioned as a lieutenant colonel in Colonel William Malcom's regiment.[319]

The rapidity of the congressional mobilization would have given George III pause, one can imagine, had he known its ultimate size. New Yorkers alone would raise about fifty thousand men for the militias and Continental forces.[320] If all the other colonies provided soldiers in the same proportion, New York's 8 to 9 percent of the population would have projected cumulative Patriot forces during the Revolution to over five hundred thousand combatants. Some New England regions, such as Connecticut, did have similar pro rata participation.

Even with redundancies of reenlistments, modern estimates place several hundred thousand in the armed forces, not including about fifty-five thousand privateers.[321] With 15 percent of the total population (or 30 percent of the male population) in arms on the Patriot side, the British had little chance to win a protracted war. Their only real chance was to annihilate an organized, armed resistance as quickly as possible—perhaps in the first year or two. To that end, George III sent Britain's largest expeditionary force of the eighteenth century to New York. About thirty-two thousand troops disembarked to Staten Island by August 1776. By mid-September, they had wrested Long Island and most of Manhattan from Washington's army.

Congress responded to the early British successes in New York by increasing the proposed size of the army from 88 regiments to 110, about ninety thousand men in 1777.[322] Although the army never reached the full measure of this plan, it showed congress did not underestimate the task ahead. It began raising an army with recruitment goals for the states that would, if filled, result in an army capable of resisting the British incursion.

During the planning phase for 1777, Washington surveyed his Continental and state militia forces to find his best officers. Colonel William Malcolm and the other officers of his regiment were generally ranked as good officers and as being in good health. Unfortunately, Isaac Stoutenburgh was apparently suffering from ill health and reported being "sickly."[323] That may have been the result of his taking on too many disparate responsibilities. While in Malcolm's regiment, he also served in the provincial congress and state senate, which would mean, if he attended all the sessions, numerous trips riding to and from wherever the congress or senate was meeting in the middle of New York in the middle of winter. The state senate of which he was a member from 1778 to 1782 had sessions in January through March in Albany, Poughkeepsie or Kingston.[324] Even today, with interstate highways, this can be rough travel in winter.

THE FDNY REBUILDS: 1777

With Isaac and sixty or so other firemen in the field serving the Patriot cause, it fell to John Dash, George Stanton and the other firemen who remained in the city to protect it from fire. Historians who confidently reported that every fireman in the city joined Washington's army were largely silent on how fires were fought during the war without a fire department, perhaps imagining that the British military establishment spontaneously mustered for fires during the war. But as previously noted, the FDNY was in the city and active from 1777 to 1783. Especially after 1778, it was the city's principal firefighting force, although British troops and auxiliaries often supplemented their efforts.

Beginning in 1777, the department rebuilt around its core veterans. There was no shortage of civilians, as thirty thousand people migrated to the city to avoid the calamity of war.[325] Even close to the city, in New Jersey, Westchester and Long Island, there were raids by "militias" from both sides, burning barns and homes—a civil war of Americans, vindictive and ugly. General Robertson, commanding military law in the city, did not hesitate to recruit a watch from the city's burgeoning numbers, a nightly force of eighty that was three times the size of the city's peacetime watch.[326]

In 1777, as New York more than replaced its prewar population, the fire department responded to several fires—two in January destroyed the Skinner House near the military warehouse and Samuel Deal's House on Duke Street; two fires in February were quenched quickly and caused little damage, while another house in February was severely damaged. The response by the FDNY during this time would seem to be similar to its response in the prewar years. If they caught a fire early, as they did in the mid-February hearth and chimney fires, little damage was done. If alarmed later, the house would usually be burned down, but they would be able to prevent the fire from spreading to adjacent houses.

THE FIRE OF 1778

In 1778, there were no newsworthy fires until August. Then all hell broke loose. On Monday night, August 3, around 1:00 a.m., a house on Cruger's Wharf near Old Slip Market burst into flames. At first, it swept away the long quadrangle block of houses, stores and warehouses from the water line to Little Dock Street. Three ships at the docks were also destroyed. The fire then crossed Little Dock Street and began to burn its other side. Soon, the fire jumped to Greater Dock Street, where the fire consumed another block of buildings and headed southwest toward the fish market. The fire was stopped at Isaac Low's house, which was still severely damaged. Only

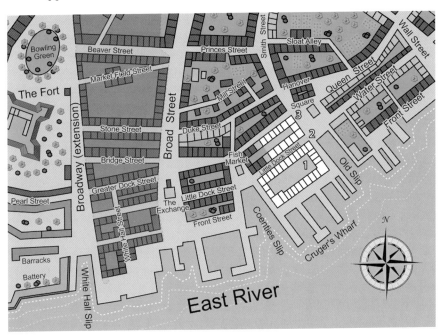

The 1778 fire began near Old Slip at Cruger's Wharf (1), then jumped over Little Dock Street (2) and down that block (3). Sixty-four houses and several ships and warehouses were destroyed. It was the second-worst fire in colonial New York.

a half dozen buildings remained intact on the block between Greater and Little Dock Streets. The fire was also stopped before it crossed Greater Dock Street, avoiding a catastrophe like that seen in 1776.[327]

While it was not on the scale of the 1776 fire, the most destructive fire in colonial North America, the fire of 1778 was disastrous enough. Sixty to seventy buildings were destroyed, mostly houses in a city that already had a severe housing shortage from the fire twenty-three months before. The fire also consumed an army warehouse with four weeks' supply of goods for the tens of thousands of British soldiers who were then in America, including thirty thousand blankets and ten thousand uniforms. The destruction was estimated at £250,000 ($40–$50 million in the twenty-first century).[328]

Nothing in the newspapers explained why the fire was not stopped earlier. Certainly, fire engines and firemen could have responded to the blaze within the first hour. However, by inference from what the British commander ordered shortly after the fire, it is probable that some well-meaning but inexperienced British officers took it upon themselves to "manage" fighting the fire to the detriment of the veteran firefighters on the ground. According to David Grim, a witness who drew maps of the fires of 1776 and 1778:

> *The cause of so many houses being burned at this time was the military officers taking* [away] *the ordering and directions of this fire from the firemen. The citizens complained thereof, to the commander-in-chief, who immediately gave general orders that, in future, no military man should interfere with any fire that may happen in the city and leave the extinguishing thereof to the entire directions of the firemen and inhabitants.*[329]

Thus, from the perspective of the FDNY, the 1778 fire resulted in the department unequivocally in charge of firefighting in the city of New York. There is no record of an organization chart of the department to show how it was structured. However, General James Robertson (at first the commandant of the martial law regime in the city and later promoted to military governor) issued an official commission later in the war (1782) to five Loyalist leaders of the fire department: John Dash, George Stanton, Jeronimus Alstyne, Frances Dominick and George Wallagrave. Robertson appointed them:

> *To be the ingineers* [sic] *in and over the different fire engine companies… with full power and authority to command the…companies…and to give such orders to your formen* [sic] *and common men acting under you in time*

of fire…and authority to order to order the inhabitants…into ranks so as to supply the ingines [sic] *with water.*[330]

This appointment formally endorsed what had most likely been British de facto policy since 1778, when the department was explicitly placed in command of the city's firefighters. One reason for the timing of this official document was that the engineers needed to publicly recruit new members for the department toward the end of the war as Loyalist firemen began to leave the city. They assumed the State of New York would resume its former punitive policies against Loyalists in the clear and present future.

1779–82 FDNY

After the 1778 fire, with the department managing firefighting, the destruction by fire returned to the levels of the prewar years. For the 1779 to 1783 period, there were three or fewer fires per year, and in one year, 1781, there were no newsworthy fires. The department's effective response had returned. With the FDNY restored to productive numbers and authority, the worst fires in New York during the war were over.

A large fire in 1782 demonstrated how firefighting had evolved toward the end of the war. The fire started in a baker's shop on Wall Street, where the congestion of buildings presented the dangerous occasion for a large block fire like the one at Cruger's Wharf. The fire was stopped with the total loss of four buildings—two burned down and two pulled down—and with several others damaged. The newspaper credited the successfully contained blaze to "the friendly assistance of the military" and the exertions of the city firemen and "gentlemen of the fire club."[331]

The tearing down of buildings was undoubtedly the work of the firemen, who would keep the demolished buildings wet to provide a firebreak. The military at fires like these would contribute to the bucket brigades and might even relieve the firemen pumping the engines. The fire clubs and the gentlemen thereof had begun to protect valuable household items, such as furniture and plate, and the commercial inventories of those who subscribed to their services as early as the mid-eighteenth century.

The British military commanders in New York City during the war did not neglect firefighting or fire prevention. They increased the size and scope of the watch, empowered the experienced civilian fire department to

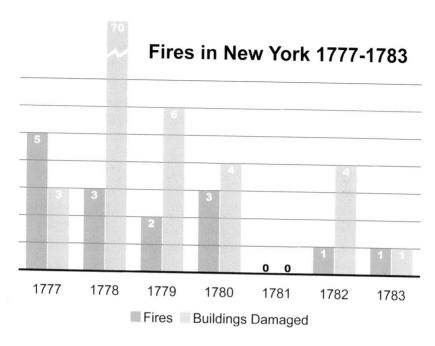

Revolutionary fires after 1778, when the British returned the authority to command the fire ground back to the FDNY. They were similar in frequency and severity to those of the prewar years.

manage the firegrounds and encouraged the fire clubs to rescue household valuables and commercial inventories from incineration. They also enforced ordinances that chimneys be swept and imposed fines on those who, through negligence, had chimney fires.[332] And significantly, they provided for the purchase and maintenance of fire buckets and fire engines.

The British created a lottery in 1780 to raise money to buy buckets.[333] That same year, they had already demonstrated the efficacy of two lotteries to raise funds for the homeless poor, who had been streaming into New York for three years.[334] Lotteries contributed over £10,000 to the budget of the city from 1777 to 1782, 16 percent of the total. The largest revenue source, over 70 percent, was the "rents of houses" from abandoned properties of both Patriots and Loyalists who were no longer in the city. Ferry rents, liquor licenses and fines comprised the remaining 12 percent of the city funding.[335]

The bulk of these funds for the five-year period, about 60 percent, went to the support of the poor, including the Alms House. The repairs of fire engines shared an expense category that contained repairs of buildings, ferries, pumps and lamps, about £4,262 or 7 percent of the total. Although not listed in the newspaper summary as a separate line item, with just £300, the city could have bought three engines and repaired a half dozen more.[336] Perhaps the emphasis here should not be on exactly how much the city spent on fire engines but on the fact that the city had the funds and more than enough motivation to invest in as many fire engines, buckets and firefighting tools as they felt necessary. They also had the skilled fire engineers to build, maintain and deploy them.

Although the wartime FDNY may have had a capability like that of the prewar years, it did not enjoy the tranquility of the peacetime city. Beginning with the fire of 1776, the British military feared incendiary raids from the Patriot militias, mainly in the suburbs of Westchester County and Long Island, and pro-Patriot arsonists in the city itself. In establishing the eighty-man watch in 1777, the British commandant Robertson proclaimed, "There is ground to believe that the rebels, not satisfied with the destruction of part of the city, entertain designs of burning the rest."[337] Any large fire, such as the one at Cruger's Wharf, provoked suspicion and scrutiny. In 1779, rumors of "several hundred rebel conspirators who intend to set fire to the city" initiated arrests and caused "much anxiety in the soldiers in New York."[338] A year later, the British commandant offered a fifty-guinea reward for information leading to the arrest of arsonists planning an attack on the city's arsenals, an attempt he thought imminent.[339]

Adding to the anxiety in 1780 was a fire in the harbor, reported at first in a "hospital ship" accidentally burning to the water line in Wallabout Bay (off Brooklyn). In fact, the ship, *Good Hope*, although sounding like a benign sentiment, was not a hospital ship but a prison ship. And it did not burn accidentally but through the efforts of captured Patriot prisoners on board who were led by a Connecticut man named Woodberry.[340] According to David Sproat, a Philadelphia Loyalist merchant dispossessed of his fortune by the war and then the British commissary of prisoners, the prisoners "maliciously and wickedly burnt the best prison ship in the world." Nearby British transports rescued almost all of the several hundred prisoners; only two were missing.[341] Since British prisons were notorious for horrific conditions resulting in starvation, disease and death, in addition to cruel beatings and arbitrary murder, it is surprising the British did not hang Woodberry and his fellow incendiaries but confined them in the Provost Jail. Perhaps burning one's own prison ship was so without precedent that they had no established punishment for it.

The year 1781, the year after the Good Hope fire, was exceptional in the recorded annals of New York in that it had no newsworthy fires— that is, none that appeared in the newspapers. It did not take a big or particularly damaging fire to get into print. New York papers regularly reported small, contained chimney fires alongside conflagrations in London or Constantinople. But 1781 was the first year in twenty that there were no significant fires—another indication that the fire department and fire prevention had returned to its prewar form.

FDNY Management at War's End

The five-engineer FDNY management organized or reorganized several engine companies before the end of the war.[342] With twelve engines at the beginning of the war, an engine company need not have been organized around a new piece of equipment, just one perhaps that had not been deployed. Since there was very little left to burn after the 1776/1778 blazes in large parts of the West, South, and Dock Wards, the department may have mothballed some of their engines and assigned their trained firemen to fill the shortages in other companies.

Following what must have been a routine procedure by 1780, the department formed a new engine company, later designated No. 11-Oceanus, around a core of five Loyalist veterans. Daniel Ten Eyck, the foreman, had been a Dock Ward fireman for over a decade. Other Dock Warders joined him. Also represented in the company were a new generation of the sons and nephews of firemen, legacies from families like the Ten Eyck, Wessels and Moores.[343] Another fifteen recruits filled the roster and would remain in decade-long service. By the end of the war, the department reported fourteen engine companies, although some engines needed repairs.

It took some effort for the five engineers managing the department to maintain the rosters of the expanded companies. Upon learning

WHEREAS there are a number of FIRE-MEN now wanted to fill up the different vacancies in the Companies belonging to the Fire Engines in this city, occasioned by a number of men belonging to the said Companies removing to other parts; it is hereby requested by the Engineers, that any person or persons, residents in this City, that they are requested to apply immediately, in order that the said Companies may have their full compliment of men. None need apply but those who are sober, discreet persons. Enquire of said Engineers, who are appointed by Authority for that purpose.

John B. Dash,
George Stanton,
Francis Deminkel,
Jeronimus Uline,
George Walligrave.

A 1783 advertisement for firemen, highlights the departure of many firefighters who feared the new American regime.

the terms of the peace, many of the Loyalist firemen began to leave the city. In August 1783, the engineers advertised in the newspaper. Since all five engineers listed their names in the advertisement, they were all still active in the management of the department just a few months before the November evacuation of the British.[344]

THE LOYALIST ENGINEERS PROPOSAL FOR A POSTWAR FDNY

Just after the evacuation, the fire engineers, managers of the department since 1778, made a written proposal to George Clinton, who, as governor, was the highest-ranking official in the State of New York. One engineer's name is missing in that proposal, George Waldegrove (also spelled Wallegrove, Walligrave, Wallagrave, Walgrove and Walgrave in newspapers and fire company rosters over the previous twenty years). Waldegrove had been a fireman in the prewar department from at least 1754 and was the foreman of a West Ward company by 1772. The Sons of Liberty noted George's political tendency and placed him on the 1770 pro-importation list (as Walgrove). The Committee of Safety confiscated his guns before the war (as Wollegrove), as they had Dash's and other "suspected" Loyalists. As a foreman of one of the larger engine companies in the West Ward, it was perhaps natural for him to take a leadership position in the department when the war began. He was still active as one of the five managing engineers at the end of the war, but for whatever reasons, he did not sign the proposal for a postwar fire department. Perhaps he wanted to see how the new government would treat Loyalists. Would the "Committee of Safety" be reborn to monitor and prosecute former political opponents?

The trend of New York state legislation in the war years was less than favorable for the Loyalists. The Banishing Act, the Forfeitures Act, the Act of Attainder, the Citation Act and the Trespass Act were disestablishing virtually every political, civil and property right that thousands of Loyalists formerly enjoyed. The Act of Attainder itself demonized fifty-nine prominent citizens, pronounced them guilty of treason, seized their estates and mandated their execution if captured; 1,500 more estates were confiscated, and hundreds were banished.[345] Since these plaintive engineers were Loyalists and had publicly exhibited Loyalist sentiments, they could very easily end up on the wrong side of one of the New York State acts, risking banishment, at least, if not a more severe retribution.

and preservation of . his Metropolis at Times depend greatly in keeping the Engines in good Order.

We no beg leave to inform your Excellency, that we held a Commission Jointly and Severally, under the late Governor *Robertson*, and are happy to say we always gain'd applause from the Citizens for Our good Conduct in the Alarming time of Fire in this City — Should it please your Excellency to Continue us in this office under your Administration we will always Act with such Conduct, as we make no Doubt will, when Called upon in Time of Fire gain the applause of your Excellency, as well as in the late Fire we have of the Citizens. —— We

Remain with Great Respect

Your Excellency's Most Obed. &

Most Hum.ble Servts.

John Balthazer Dash.

George Stanton

Francis Dominick

Jeronemus Alstyne &

New york 27th November 1783.

The 1783 proposal (segment here) from Loyalist engineers who led the wartime FDNY was sent to George Clinton, New York's governor, with plans to form and manage the department after the war.

Seeing only an alarmingly dangerous future in Revolutionary America, over ten thousand Loyalists did depart New York in 1783.

It is therefore not surprising that one of the engineers who managed the department during the war decided to adopt a lower public profile after the war. The transition to a new government was fraught with uncertainty. What is surprising, however, is that four of the engineers were not on the boats for Nova Scotia or England. They decided to stay. Not only did they stay, but they publicly proposed to organize and manage the postwar fire department in New York, even as the new civil government was being formed.

In their proposal, their rationale to manage the department was simple enough. They were competent: "We always gained the applause from the citizens for our good conduct in the alarming times of fire in the city." They were ready: "We will always act with such conduct, as we…no doubt will, when called upon in the time of fire, gain the applause of your excellency." And they knew, in detail, what equipment and repairs needed "immediate dispatch." "We think it our duty and therefore take this early opportunity to represent this matter to your excellency, as the safety and preservation of this metropolis, at times, depend greatly on keeping the engines in good order."[346]

After their signatures on the proposal, the engineers listed fourteen engine companies and two hook-and-ladder companies, along with the foreman for each company. They also specified the number of men each engine would need. In total, there would be 253 firefighters for this expanded department, about 80 more than before the war. It is doubtful that they had over 200 firemen at the end of 1783, but with Patriot firemen returning to the city, they could project a force of that size with some confidence.

The Early Post-Revolution FDNY

A few days after the engineers' proposal, an interim city "council" set up by the state responded. They appointed John Dash as "superintendent" of the fire engines and enjoined him to put them in good order and repair as soon as possible. They also certified that the engineers and firemen who were then serving would remain in their positions until the city council made any changes.[347] As a result, the engineers' proposal was accepted for the time being, and Dash and his crew began making repairs on the engines where necessary. It was clearly a temporary measure, but it was a lot better than being banished. How long the honeymoon would last between the new civil government and the existing Loyalist-managed fire department was still anybody's guess.

The Loyalist engineers had organized their proposed fire department around their prewar firefighting colleagues, half of their designated foremen being firefighters before the war.[348] However, although Dash was placed in charge of the engines for a while, the initiative by the Loyalist engineers to remain the leaders of the fire department was short-lived. Governor Clinton, following provincial precedents, delegated the management of the New York Fire Department to the city's newly reformed common council.

The common council met one month after the letter to Clinton and appointed William J. Elsworth, who had been in the Patriot military, as its new head engineer. Thus, Elsworth, who had been a veteran fireman and engine company foreman, also had revolutionary credentials that were more congenial to the political climate of the time. The council then endorsed Elsworth's slate of assistants—John Stagg, Francis Bassett, Isaac Mead and John Quackenboss—whose Patriotic credentials were also in order.[349]

Elsworth was able to reconstitute the department in 1784 around a core of department veterans. About sixty firefighters from the 1770s appeared on the department roles in the 1780s.[350] Most of the reorganized companies were at full force by the end of 1784. A large part of the city was still in ashes and would take a decade to rebuild. About 40 percent of its prewar population of twenty-five thousand were refugees, mostly in Canada. But the fire department was not only intact but more robust than ever within a few months, ready to grow with New York and the new America.[351]

EPILOGUE

John B. Dash delivered fourteen engines (two more than he had received in 1776) to the new foremen of the fire companies, then retired from active service.[352] However, his son John B. Dash Jr. continued the family tradition of fire service, becoming a foreman and eventually an assistant engineer. Stanton would serve as a fire warden, an assessor and an inspector of elections in the 1780s. George Dominick became an assessor in the mid-1780s, and Jeronimus Alstine became a fire warden, also in the 1790s. Thus, the Loyalist engineers seemed to be integrated back into civic and social life soon after the end of the war, although not as leaders of the fire department they had managed during the war.

Jacobus Stoutenburgh died in his mid-seventies during the war somewhere outside the city. With little or no notice of his death during the war, it was not until after the war that his will was read, and his family went on with their lives.[353] He did not live to see fire department as it emerged from the Revolution, but he would have recognized it. It was his assistants and foremen from his tenure before the war who had protected the city for eight years during the war. The legacy he left the people of New York lasted well into the middle of the next century. It was the essential organization of the Fire Department of New York—a chief engineer and several assistants managing fire companies, with a foreman for each engine and a band of highly motivated volunteers. Moreover, with his tenure of over forty years and his crucial contributions to the department during that time, Jacobus Stoutenburgh could properly be called the father of the FDNY.

Jacobus Stoutenburgh's nephew Isaac was a fireman by 1762 and became his assistant in the fire department in 1769. Isaac joined the Revolutionary cause early. In 1775, he formed a New York City militia company, which, as it merged with other companies, became a battalion that later grew into a regiment. By 1776, he was commissioned as a lieutenant colonel.[354] Coincident with his military career, his political career began in 1775–77, with his election to the Second and Third Provincial Congresses and later to the state senate from 1778 to 1787.[355]

After the war, Governor Clinton appointed Isaac as a commissioner of forfeitures, whose job it was to liquidate the confiscated estates of Loyalists. The largest estate he liquidated was that of Philipse Manor, which included the towns of Yonkers, Greenburgh, Mount Pleasant and Ossining. Stoutenburgh reported sales of £502,709 for the district. That is about $100,000,000 in the twenty-first century, a few orders of magnitude lower than their present value.[356]

From 1789 to 1795, Isaac served as an alderman from the West Ward for the City of New York, which was still rebuilding the ground of its war losses from the two large fires in 1776 and 1778. Isaac himself managed the planning, surveying and building projects of several city streets.[357] Before and after his tenure as an alderman, he did contract work for the city, building bulkheads for the Cortlandt, Dey and Veseys Slips, several iron monger projects, and managed the building of Newgate Prison. He died in 1799.[358]

Isaac was a fourth-generation American Stoutenburgh. His father, a gunsmith and a fireman, had served on the common council and managed dozens of public works, along with the colonial night watch, for decades. His uncle Jacobus, also a gunsmith, was the city's first engineer (fire chief) and oversaw the growth and "modernization" of the fire department. This Isaac Stoutenburgh was also a gunsmith and fireman. He raised a militia company, participated in the early provincial and state governments, liquidated the massive Loyalist estates, served the city as an alderman and managed large civic projects. He contributed substantially to the distinguished Stoutenburgh legacy in eighteenth-century New York.

The Stoutenburgh legacy has only been partially recalled here. Mentioned in part I of this book is the fantastic story of the original American Stoutenburgh, Pieter, who possibly had a Dutch heritage worthy of royalty. It is a story that has been recounted more fully on the Saving New York (www.savingny.com) website. It may be apocryphal—that is, it may not be true—but it should be. Also on the website is the strange tale of Cornelis van Tienhoven coming back from Amsterdam with a mistress. His wife, Rachel,

Advanced Dutch firefighting used high-pressure hoses connected to engines that were then hauled close to fires to spray directly on them. Colonial New York used similar engines, but they did not have high-pressure hoses.

and three children awaited to greet his ship on its arrival in Manhattan—surprises likely for many.

Among the many interesting website additions to the history of firefighting is the extended narrative of Van Der Heyden, the Dutch artist and engineer. He was a century ahead of his time in making and using a practical leather hose. He attached high-pressure hoses directly to the engines so that they could be extended to get streams directly on fires inside buildings and their upper stories.

Finally, a little after the period covered in this book was the extraordinary story of how Aaron Burr hoodwinked the entire Federalist establishment, especially Alexander Hamilton. Burr proposed a corporation to build reservoirs and water conduits to bring much-needed water from the north into the city. It, of course, would extend the essential supply of water for firefighting. The Federalists thought they were getting a company to provide the water the city needed to protect itself, grow and prosper. What they got was the first Republican-controlled bank in New York.

These stories, some suitable for Broadway musicals, and more can be found at www.savingny.com.

NOTES

Introduction

1. Dana, *Firemen*, 23, 40, 75, 184, 198, 222, 224, 229, 250, 265 (large fires in ten of the larger colonial towns); Grim, *Collections*, 276 ("The number of houses that were burned and destroyed in the city at that awful conflagration were…493").
2. Burrows and Wallace, *Gotham*, 227.
3. See "Summary Table of Carleton Commission Testimonies," Saving New York, www.savingny.com, for testimony regarding vandals and arsonists.
4. Seventeen percent, plus or minus 5 percent (Howe, "Material City").
5. See historians' views at "Web Appendix #S3: Summary Views from Principal Historians—The Cause and Culpability of the Great New York Fire of 1776," Saving New York, www.savingny.com.
6. The Carleton Commission testimonies can be found at "Carleton Commission on the Great Fire of New York in 1776 (Dated 1783)," Saving New York, www.savingny.com. A reference table for each data point shown in the map can be found at "Appendix #25: Map of Combustibles References," Saving New York, www.savingny.com.
7. Limpus, *History*, 77–80; Costello, *Our Firemen*, 39.

8. See part 3 in the section labeled "1779–1782 FDNY" for information on how lotteries funded the fire department during the American Revolution.
9. For references for Revolutionary fires, fires in New York 1777–83, see "Appendix #28: Fires in New York 1777–1783," Saving New York, www.savingny.com.
10. For map references, see "Appendix #8: A Map of New York City Wards (References," Saving New York, www.savingny.com, and for model references, visit "Appendix #4: The Roelantsen House circa 1640," Saving New York, www.savingny.com, and "Appendix #14: Newsham Engine circa 1730," Saving New York, www.savingny.com.

Chapter 1

11. For a background of WIC, see "Dutch West India Company," Wikipedia, www.en.wikipedia.org.
12. "VOC" was the abbreviation of its Dutch name, *Vereenigde Oostindische Compagnie*. The official WIC designation was *Geoctrooieerde Westindische Compagnie*, chartered West India Company.
13. "Money Substitutes in New Netherland and Early New York: The Beaver Pelt," Department of Special Collections, University of Notre Dame Libraries, Coin and Currency Collections, www.coins.nd.edu; for an extensive discussion of wampum, see "Money Substitutes in New Netherland and Early New York: Wampum," Department of Special Collections, University of Notre Dame Libraries, Coin and Currency Collections, www.coins.nd.edu; Maika, "Commerce and Community"; Peña, "Wampum Production."
14. See "Appendix #3: Guilders, Pelts, Wampum... The Cost of Food & Clothing in New Amsterdam," Saving New York, www.savingny.com.
15. Burrows and Wallace, *Gotham*, 37–38.
16. Kessler and Rachlis, *Peter Stuyvesant*, 55–60.
17. Jacobs, "Early Years," 229–31.
18. Ibid., 31–235; Jacobs, *New Netherland*, 63; Burrows and Wallace, *Gotham*, 41; Kessler and Rachlis, *Peter Stuyvesant*, 45, 46, 287.
19. Kessler and Rachlis, *Peter Stuyvesant*, 46–47.
20. Ibid., 47.
21. Ibid., 49.

22. See Shorto's *The Island at the Center of the World* for more information on the leader of this anti-WIC/anti-Stuyvesant faction, Adrian van der Donck.

23. Jacobs, *New Netherland*, 406.

24. *Historical Manuscripts*, 2:13–14. The cost was 350 Carolus guilders, Holland currency.

25. Fernow, *Records of New Amsterdam*, 1:5.

26. Ibid.

27. Pincus, *Protestantism and Patriotism*, 83–97.

28. Fernow, *Records of New Amsterdam*, 1:65.

29. Ibid.,1:65–67.

30. Ibid., 1:72–74 (elaborates on an original palisade design and its replacement by the plank design); see "Web Appendix #5: The Palisade Wall and The Plank Wall," Saving New York, www.savingny.com, for references and conversions from Dutch to metric or English measures.

31. Fernow, *Records of New Amsterdam*, 1:182.

32. *DRCH*, 1:317.

33. The faction's early success was due to Tienhoven's disappearance at a critical juncture in the proceedings. The details of Thienhoven's aberrant behavior are in *DRCH*, 1:514–17.

34. O'Callaghan, *Register*, 173–74.

35. Jacobs, "Early Years," 170–71.

36. Burrows and Wallace, *Gotham*, 68.

37. Kessler and Rachlis, *Peter Stuyvesant*, 160–64.

38. Ibid., 165–68.

39. Fernow, *Records of New Amsterdam*, 1:374.

40. Ibid., 1:366.

41. Historical Society of New York Courts, "Legal History Matters," www.nycourts.gov.

42. Fernow, *Records of New Amsterdam*, 1:35.

43. Modeled on civil governance in Amsterdam, burghers were colonists with civil and commercial privileges as described previously. Great burghers, the wealthier colonists, had extended judicial rights and could participate in higher levels of civil governance.

44. Fernow, *Records of New Amsterdam*, 1:35.

45. Ibid., 7:191.

46. Ibid., 7:207, 209.

47. Ibid., 1:5.

48. Ibid., 7:195.

49. Costello, *Our Firemen*, 9–12.
50. United States Census Bureau, "Population in the Colonial and Continental Priods," 11, www.census.gov.
51. Boston History and Architecture, "Population Trends in Boston 1640–1990," www.iboston.org.
52. Broad Street had a canal down its center for several decades until Governor Andros had it filled in in the 1670s.
53. Peterson, "New York," 172–74.
54. A scenario from *Broadside*. See "The Story of *Broadside*," youdoc, www.youtube.com.
55. *DRCH*, 2:445–46.
56. For the extended description of the governmental functions in New Netherlands, see Jacobs, "Early Years," 95–189. For the period between 1655 and 1675 in New Amsterdam, Jacobs, "Early Years," 165–89.
57. *DRCH*, 2:376.
58. Ibid., 2:248–49.
59. Ibid., 3:57 ("'Private Instructions to Coll. R. Nicolls &c,' a Letter from Charles the Second…to Nicolls and Other Commissioners Enjoined to Takeover All New Netherland Including Long Island").
60. For extensive discussion of wampum see "Money Substitutes in New Netherland and Early New York: Wampum"; Maika, "Commerce and Community"; Peña, "Wampum Production."
61. Israel, *Dutch Republic*, 774. See "Appendix #7: Why the Dutch Gave up New Netherland," Saving New York, www.savingny.com, for the Dutch rationale of relinquishing the colony to the English.
62. Kessler and Rachlis, *Peter Stuyvesant*, 278–80.
63. Brindenbaugh, *Cities*, 68.
64. Fernow, *Records of New Amsterdam*, 1:21–22; Costello, *Our Firemen*, 11.

Chapter 2

65. United States Census Bureau, "Population," 11.
66. See Appendix S2, "How the Glorious Revolution Came to America," Saving New York, https://www.savingny.com/appendices1.html.
67. Ritchie, *Duke's Province*, 41.
68. Ibid., 27, 41–47; Burrows and Wallace, *Gotham*, 78.
69. Ritchie, *Duke's Province*, 27.
70. Costello, *Our Firemen*, 19.

71. Schomette and Haslach, *Raid on America*, 95–110, 169–74.

72. Harding, *Seapower*, 104.

73. Schomette and Haslach, *Raid on America*, 292–95. The principle for a treaty that kept whatever was gained during the war also had a Latin name, *uti possidetis*, which just goes to show that whenever politicians begin to use Latin, hold on to your wallet.

74. Schomette and Haslach, *Raid on America*, 172. "It was said that the Dutch expended 2,000 rounds against the fortress before the fight was through."

75. *MCCCNY*, 1:42 (1676).

76. Peterson, "New York," 176.

77. Archdeacon, *New York City*, 102–4; Burrows and Wallace, *Gotham*, 91–92.

78. Stone, *History*, 70.

79. Ibid., 70–71.

80. *MCCCNY*, 1:147.

81. Peterson, "New York," 63–166.

82. *MCCCNY*, 1:139.

83. Ibid., 1:187.

84. Ibid., 1:178–79.

85. Archdeacon, *New York City*, 83.

86. *MCCCNY*, 1:259.

87. Burrows and Wallace, *Gotham*, 110.

88. Wayne Andrews, "A Glance at New York in 1697: The Travel Diary of Dr. Benjamin Bullivant," *New York Historical Society Quarterly* 40 (January 1956): 55–73.

89. Knight, *Private Journal*, 66–68.

90. Brayley, *Complete History*, 16.

91. Howe, "Material City," 6.

92. United States Census Bureau, "Population," 11.

93. Burrows and Wallace, *Gotham*, 85.

94. *MCCCNY*, 1:427.

95. Ibid., 2:23–24.

Chapter 3

96. *DRCH*, 1:395–420. See "Appendix #9: Population, Houses, Households Circa 1700," Saving New York, www.savingny.com, for a comprehensive discussion of the 1703 census.

97. See "Appendix #11: Slaveholding by Class Circa 1700" (Saving New York, www.savingny.com) for a projection of slavery by household assets.

98. The census of 1703 listings denote 18 percent of the population as enslaved and living in the households. See "Appendix #9: Population, Houses, Households circa 1700," Saving New York, www.savingny.com; and "Appendix #11: Slaveholding by Class Circa 1700," Saving New York, www.savingny.com.
99. *CLONY*, 1:764–65.
100. Ibid., 1:765–66.
101. Ibid., 1:761–67.
102. Ibid., 5:341 (From a letter from Hunter to the Lords of Trade, June 23, 1712).
103. Ibid.
104. Aptheker, *Slave Revolts*, 18–52.
105. "Mr. Bradford," *NYG*, March 24, 1734, 1.
106. Ibid.
107. Hough, *Census*, iv–v.
108. See "Appendix #9: Population, Houses, Households circa 1700," Saving New York, www.savingny.com, for links to the number of enslaved children tabulated in 1703 New York City census.
109. Goodfriend, *Melting Pot*, 155; Hough, *Census*, iv–v.
110. Goodfriend, *Melting Pot*, 62, 156–57.
111. Aptheker, *Slave Revolts*, 144–46. The American Fire Insurance Company of Philadelphia stopped writing policies in the slaveholding South by 1820.
112. "Hamburgh," *NYG*, August 23, 1731, 2.
113. "Boston," *NYG*, January 7, 1734, 2.
114. Lepore, *New York Burning*, 903–5.
115. *MCCCNY*, 4:56.
116. Woodcroft, *Appendix*, 69: A.D. 1725, no. 479. Records Newsham's updated patent in 1725. Newsham's original patent was granted in 1721 (no. 439, "Newsham, *Engine for Extinguishing Fires*").
117. The *NYG* published an account of the engines being shipped from London on page 2 of its November 22, 1731 edition. It noted the engines were of the second and fifth sizes.
118. Switzer, *General System*, 3:351–54. In his "Notes to Vol III," Switzer reproduced contemporary promotional material from both Newsham and his chief rival, Mr. Fowke of Nightingale, Wapping.
119. See "Appendix #13: A Newsham Broadside," Saving New York, www.savingny.com, for the specifications of the Newsham and Fowke engines.

120. Cannon, *Heritage*, 118–20 (reproductions of diagrams of a then-modern Newsham engine, detailing its refinements from the mid-eighteenth century).

121. Woodcroft, *Appendix*, 66: A.D. 1724, no. 466. The record of the original patent (not by Newsham) on which Newsham based his novel gearing used in his contemporary engines.

122. Ingram, *History*, 10–11.

123. Assuming Newsham's engines could throw a stream forty yards, the height of the stream would be high enough for virtually all of the houses—but perhaps not the church steeples or fort buildings.

124. *MCCCNY*, 4:149. The exact payment to DeLancey and Moore was £204.12 in the currency of New York, not quite as much as London pounds, which would be closer to ⅔ of that amount or £140. According to "Currency Conversion (University of Wyoming, www.uwyo.edu), 1 British pound in 1730, was equal to about $200 in the twenty-first century.

125. "London, September 10," *NYG*, November 22, 1731, 2; "Coum House, New-York, Inward Entries," *NYG*, December 6, 1731, 2.

126. Costello, *Our Firemen*, 26; *Boston Weekly Newsletter,* January 6, 1732.

127. "As Fire is a Good Servant," *NYG*, December 21, 1731, 1.

128. *MCCCNY*, 4:175.

129. Ibid., 4:168.

130. Ibid.

131. "New-York, March 20," *NYG*, March 20, 1733, 2.

132. "New-York," *NYG*, December 17, 1733, 2.

133. Ibid.

134. "New-York, December 22," *NYG*, December 23, 1735, 4.

135. "New-York, Jan. 21," *NYG*, January 20, 1736, 4.

136. *MCCCNY*, 4:175.

137. Costello, *Our Firemen*, 27.

138. *MCCCNY*, 4:367.

139. "New York," *NYG*, January 4, 1737, 4.

140. "New-York, January 18," *NYG*, January 18, 1737, 4.

141. *MCCCNY*, 4:437–38.

142. Ibid.

143. Stoutenburgh-Teller Family Association, "Descendants of Pieter Stoutenburg: Generation 1," www.stoutenburgh.com.

144. Ibid.

145. Cannon, *Heritage*, 157.

146. Ibid., 29.

147. "Spectator, No. 427," *NYG*, March 18, 1734, 2; "Mr. Bradford," *NYG*, March 25, 1734, 1.
148. "New-York," *NYG*, September 19, 1737, 3.

Chapter 4

149. *DRCH*, 6:186 (Letter from Lieutenant Governor George Clarke to the Lords of Trade, April 22, 1741).
150. Horsmanden, *New-York Conspiracy*, 24.
151. *DRCH*, 6:188 (Letter from Lieutenant Governor George Clarke to the Duke of Newcastle, May 15, 1741).
152. Horsmanden, *Journal*, 25.
153. Ibid., 8.
154. Rabin, *New York Conspiracy*, 113.
155. Horsmanden, *Journal*, 28.
156. Ibid.
157. Ibid., 29.
158. Ibid., 32.
159. Ibid.
160. Lepore, *New York Burning*, 1,594–95.
161. Horsmanden, *Journal*, 27.
162. Horsmanden's case against Ury depended on the testimonies of Mary Burton, the soldier William Kane and Sarah Hughson, the daughter of John Hughson.
163. Burrows and Wallace, *Gotham*, 163–64.
164. Ibid., 163.
165. *MCCCNY*, 5:22.
166. Burrows and Wallace, *Gotham*, 165.
167. *MCCCNY*, 5:43.
168. Ibid., 5:54.
169. See "Appendix #16: Night Watch/Lighting Expenditures," Saving New York, www.savingny.com, for references.
170. *MCCCNY*, 5:77.
171. Ibid., 5:100.
172. Stoutenburgh-Teller Family Association, "Descendants," www.stoughtenburgh.com.
173. *MCCCNY*, 5:1–2.

Chapter 5

174. "New-York, January 26," *NYG-P*, no. 210 (January 26, 1747): 3.
175. Alternatively, the ship could have been close enough to shore, say forty yards, for one of the larger engines to play on it from shore. But many city ordinances (see vols. 5 and 6 of *MCCCNY*) fined ships that stayed close to the wharves for too long, so it is doubtful that three ships, the *William* and the other two, were within spraying distance of the shore.
176. "New-York, April 4," *NYG-P*, no. 272 (April 4, 1748): 2.
177. "New-York, April 24," *NYG-P*, no. 327 (April 24, 1749): 2.
178. *MCCCNY*, 5:262–64.
179. "New-York, June 24," *NYG-P*, no. 127 (June 24, 1745): 4.
180. "New-York, January 19," *NYG-P*, no. 209 (January 19, 1747): 3.
181. "Marriage ID 2220285770, 1749," *New York Genealogical and Biographical Record* (1938): 268. www.ancestry.com.
182. Burrows and Wallace, *Gotham*, 168.
183. "New-York, June 21," *NYM*, no. 202 (June 21, 1756): 3.
184. Franklin, "Letter to William Parsons, June 28, 1756," in *Papers*, ed. Labaree, 6:465–66.
185. Burrows and Wallace, *Gotham*, 169.
186. "New-York, June 27," *NYG-P*, no. 754 (June 27, 1757): 3.
187. Ibid.
188. Anderson, *Crucible of War*, 320.
189. "New York, February 21," *NYG-P*, no. 736 (February 21, 1757): 3.
190. *CLONY*, 4:573–74.
191. "New York, February 23," *NYM*, March 1, 1762, 2.
192. Edwards, *Eighteenth-Century Municipality*, 126.
193. *MCCCNY*, 6:90.
194. Brayley, *Complete History*, 57–59.
195. *CLONY*, 4:673.
196. Ibid., 4:1,048.
197. *MCCCNY*, 7:144–46.
198. "New York, January 13," *NYM*, no. 742 (January 13, 1766): 3.
199. "New York, March 28," *NYG-WM*, no. 856 (March 28, 1768): 2.
200. "New York, March 31," *NYJ*, no. 1,317 (March 31, 1768): 3.
201. Ibid., 2.
202. "New York, September 15," *NYJ*, no. 1341 (September 15, 1768): 2–3.
203. "New York, March 15," *NYJ*, no. 1,419 (March 15, 1770): 3.

204. Letter to the editor, *NYG-P*, no. 1,422 (April 2, 1770): 1.

205. "New York, May 3." *NYG-WM*, no. 1,071 (May 4, 1772): 2.

206. *MCCCNY*, 7:385–87.

207. "New York, May 3," *NYG-WM*, no. 1,071 (May 4, 1772): 2; "Supplement," *NYG-WM*, no. 858 (April 11, 1768): 1.

208. *MCCCNY*, 7:366 (Tiller), 368 (Shipman), 377 (Hunt), 463 (Stanton), 8:13 (Stanton), 40 (Stanton).

209. Ibid., 7:463, 8:13, 40, 63, 117.

210. Ibid., 7:66, 137.

211. New York Surrogate's Court, "Wills and Administrations (New York County, New York), 1680–1804; Probate Place: New York, New York; Probate Date: April 20, 1770; Wills and Administrations, vol. 0024-0027, 1763–1771," www.ancestry.com, 381–82.

212. *MCCCNY*, 7:206.

213. *CLONY*, 4:143.

214. "New York, January 3," *NYG-WM*, no. 1,158 (January 3, 1774): 3.

215. *CLONY*, 5:614.

216. *MCCCNY*, 8:30.

Chapter 6

217. *CLONY*, 2:1,064.

218. Burrows and Wallace, *Gotham*, 216–17.

219. For general background, see "Massachusetts Government Act," Wikipedia, www.en.wikipedia.org.

220. Becker, *Eve of Revolution*, 84.

221. Burrows and Wallace, *Gotham*, 223.

222. Schecter, *Battle for New York*, 51.

223. *MCCCNY-2*, 1:88–89.

224. Burrows and Wallace, *Gotham*, 216.

225. Ibid., 227.

226. *MCCCNY*, 7:385.

227. Scott and Stryker-Rodda, *Denizations, Naturalizations, and Oaths*, 120.

228. *MCCCNY*, 6:232.

229. "John Balthus Dash," *NYM*, no. 699 (March 18, 1765): 2.

230. *MCCCNY*, 7:429.

231. *Independent Journal*, no. 116 (January 8, 1785): 1; *MCCCNY-2*, 8:214.

232. Barrett, *Old Merchants*, 109.

233. "The Managers," *NYG-WM*, no. 1,168 (March 4, 1774): 1.

234. Becker, *Eve of Revolution*, 55.

235. "Supplement," *NYG-P*, no. 1,438 (July 23, 1770): 1–2. The July 23, 1770 supplement looks like an "opinion piece" by the friends of nonimportation, rather than an editorial by the publisher of the newspaper.

236. See "Appendix #20: The 1770 List of Merchants Favoring Importation" (Saving New York, www.savingny.com) for a complete 1770 supplement.

237. *COHM*, 1:259–62.

238. *JOPC*, 1:476.

239. *COHM*, 1:340–41.

240. Becker, *History of Political Parties*, 264.

241. *JOPC*, 1:135.

242. Dawson, "Incidents," 44. See "Appendix Supplement to Part Three: The Provincial Congress and the Firemen," Saving New York, www.savingny.com, for Dawson's view of the provincial congress.

243. *COHM*, 1:137.

244. *JOPC*, 1:142.

245. See "Appendix #21: Comparison of Firemen in 1772 & 1776," Saving New York, www.savingny.com, for the lists, references, and analyses.

246. *NYIR*, 15.

247. Ibid., 11.

248. *JOPC*, 1:496.

249. "Committee Chamber," *NYJ*, no. 1751 (July 18, 1776): 4.

250. *NYIR*, 119–37.

251. Costello, *Our Firemen*, 585. Compared to lists in "Appendix #22: Firemen in Patriot Military, Loyalists, Others," Saving New York, www.savingny.com.

Chapter 7

252. Washington, "To George Washington from Major General Nathanael Greene, 5 September 1776," in *Papers*, 6:222–24.

253. National Archives, "From George Washington to Lund Washington, 6 October 1776," Founders Online, April 12, 2018, www.founders. archives.gov (original source: Washington, *Papers*, 6:493–95). In this

letter, Washington expressed that he really did want to burn the city but was restrained by Congress.

254. National Archives, "From George Washington to John Hancock, 2 September 1776," Founders Online, April 12, 2018, www.founders. archives.gov (original source: Washington, *Papers*, 6:199–201).

255. National Archives, "To George Washington from John Hancock, 3 September 1776," Founders Online, April 12, 2018, www.founders. archives.gov (original source: Washington, *Papers*, 6:207).

256. Shelton, *Jumel Mansion*, 43–45.

257. *CCR*, 64–65 (Bayard Testimony). See "Carleton Commission on the Great Fire of New York in 1776 (Dated 1783)," Saving New York, www. savingny.com, for a full transcript.

258. National Archives, "From George Washington to John Hancock, 6 September 1776," Founders Online, April 12, 2018, www.founders. archives.gov (original source: Washington, *Papers*, 6:231–33).

259. Washington, "To George Washington from Major General Nathanael Greene, 5 September 1776," in *Papers*, 6:222–24.

260. Some historians claim that Stoutenburgh became a major at the head of a battalion of firemen, but there is no record of Jacobus Stoutenburgh as an officer in either the provincial militia or Washington's Continental army as noted in *Fire of Liberty* (Carp, "The Night the Yankees Burned Broadway," 801.)

261. *CCR*, 9 (Dash testimony at Carleton Commission).

262. Burrows and Wallace, *Gotham*, 227 ("the flight of thousands of Tories"— percent that left), 229, 234 (figures for American and British armies).

263. Editorial, *NYG-WM*, September 30, 1776, 3.

264. See "Appendix #23: The Fire of 1776," Saving New York, www. savingny.com, for extensive references the on fire—many are itemized in this book. Stokes, *Iconography*, 5:1,021; *CCR*, 23–24, 37–39, 72–78.

265. Henry, *Campaign*, 200–2.

266. Burrows and Wallace, *Gotham*, 227. For example, Reverend Charles Inglis wrote a pamphlet that was critical of Thomas Paine, the ardent Patriot, called *The Deceiver Unmasked* (Charles Inglis, *The True Interest of America Impartially Stated, In Certain Strictures, On a Pamphlet Entitled Common Sense* [New York: Samuel Loudon, Printer, 1776]).

267. Moore, *Diary*, 312–13.

268. *CCR*, see transcript facsimile and transcribed testimonies at www. savingny.com/carleton1776.

269. Ibid., 1–3 (Mackenzie, Trinity on Fire Early), 4–8 (Chew, Trinity Set on Fire), 39–41 (Alstine, Trinity Fire from Lutheran), 37–39 (Shipman), 58–60 (Burns, Before Lutheran was on Fire), 44–47 (Moore), 62–63 (Clark).
270. Ronald Coleman, interview in Docema LLC documentary film, *Damrell's Fire*, Amazon Prime.
271. Jones, *History of New York*, 1:617.
272. National Archives, "Washington to Lund Washington, 6 October 1776."
273. Jones, *History of New York*, 1:615.
274. Burrows and Wallace, *Gotham*, 245.
275. Ibid., 251.
276. Shelton, *Jumel Mansion*, 47 (noted that Force's *American Archives* had deleted stories of arsonists being caught red-handed).
277. Mackenzie, *Diary*, 2:58.
278. Modern estimates of the number of houses destroyed are closer to five hundred or six hundred, rather than one thousand. But the fire was still a disaster like no other in New York's colonial history (Howe, "Material City").
279. Editorial, *NYG-WM*, September 30, 1776, 3.
280. See "Web Appendix #S3: Summary Views from Principal Historians—The Cause and Culpability of the Great New York Fire of 1776," Saving New York, www.savingny.com, for more complete views by several historians.

Chapter 8

281. A facsimile copy of the commission for the three British officers to investigate the fire can be read at "Carleton Commission on the Great Fire of New York in 1776 (Dated 1783)," Saving New York, www.savingny.com.
282. National Archives, "Account of a Conference Between Washington and Sir Guy Carleton, 6 May 1783," Founders Online, www.founders.archives.gov; National Archives, "Definitive Treaty of Peace between the United States and Great Britain, 3 September 1783," Founders Online, www.founders.archives.gov (original source: Franklin, "May 16 through September 15, 1783," in *Papers*, ed. Cohn, 40:566–75).
283. "ORDERS," *NYG-WM*, June 9, 1783, 1.
284. See "Carleton Commission on the Great Fire of New York in 1776 (Dated 1783)," Saving New York, www.savingny.com, for links to a

facsimile (photograph) of Chipman's handwritten record and a text transcription of the testimonies. The testimonies and a deposition by Charles Inglis, also linked, comprise what is referred to here as the *Carleton Commission Report* (*CCR*).

285. *CCR*, 8–12 (Dash).

286. See Chapter 9 here for the details of a plan from Dash, et alia, for the postwar department.

287. Henry, *Campaign*, v–viii.

288. Ibid., 200–2.

289. Henry, *Campaign*, 200–2.

290. *CCR*, 80–83 (Grundy).

291. Carp, "Yankees Burned Broadway," 484; Grizzard and Hoth, "Trumball to Washington," in *Papers of George Washington*.

292. Burrows, *Forgotten Patriots*, 201. Burrows estimated that as many as 15,000 to 18,000 American prisoners died during the conflict (versus 6,824 combat deaths).

293. Reported by Stephen Moulton Sr. (1735–1818) of Stafford, Connecticut, a lieutenant colonel in the Connecticut militia who was captured during the retreat from New York on September 15, 1776, the British paroled Moulton in early January 1777 (National Archives, "To George Washington from Jonathan Trumbull, Sr., 12 January 1777," Founders Online, April 12, 2018, www.founders.archives.gov [original source: Washington, *Papers*, 8:53–54]).

294. National Archives, "From George Washington to Joshua Loring, 20 January 1777," Founders Online, April 12, 2018, www.founders. archives.gov (original source: Washington, *Papers*, 8:118).

295. *CCR*, 84–85.

296. Ibid., 83–84.

297. Ibid., 8 (Chew).

298. Fox, *Four Days*, 58–60. For an example of how Sir Robert Holmes used fireships to great effect, see *A Distant Storm* (Fox, 342). For a film example of how fire ships were used by the Dutch, see the movie *Broadside* (based on the Dutch raid up the River Medway).

299. Force, *American Archives*, 2:713.

300. Heath, *Memoirs*, 63.

301. *CCR*, 42 (Bridges).

302. Ibid., 17–20 (Law).

303. National Archives, "General Orders, 29 April 1776," Founders Online, April 12, 2018, www.founders.archives.gov (original source:

Washington, *Papers*, 4:162–64); National Archives, "General Orders, 21 August 1776," Founders Online, April 12, 2018, www.founders.archives. gov (original source: Washington, *Papers*, 6:95–97; Van Dyke's Company had erected this "beautifull circular Fort" northwest of the city [now the corner of Washington and Harrison Streets]).

304. David L. Sterling, "American Prisoners of War in New York: A Report by Elias Boudinot," *William and Mary Quarterly* 13, no. 3 (July 1956): 388.

305. *CCR*, 18 (Law).

306. Ibid., 15, 59. One of the testimonies of the report say Van Dyke hid in a shed rather than a closet, but Van Dyke said he hid in the house. See also Sterling, "American Prisoners of War," 388.

307. National Archives, "To George Washington from Elias Boudinot, 22 April 1778," Founders Online, April 12, 2018, www.founders.archives. gov (original source: Washington, *Papers*, 14:583–84).

308. Van Buskirk, *Generous Enemies*, 73–82.

309. Shelton suggests that this was possible (*Jumel Mansion*, 60–66).

310. Bakeless, *Turncoats*, 112–20.

311. Editorial, *NYG-WM*, September 30, 1776, 3.

312. There was at the time some confusion with this William Smith being the brother of Abigail Adams, wife of John Adams. However, Abigail's brother William was, at the time, seeking an officer's commission, still in Massachusetts. See Hafner, *William Smith*, 103–10; Shelton, *Jumel Mansion*, 44–46.

313. See "Comfort Sands," Wikipedia, www.wikipedia.org.

314. *CCR*, 8 (Dash), 28 (Sands), 52 (Stoutenburgh).

315. Ibid., 68 (Ellsworth).

316. Ibid., 68.

Chapter 9

317. *CCR*, 9–12 (Dash).

318. See "Appendix #20: Firemen in Patriot Military, Loyalists, Others," Saving New York, www.fdnyandtheamericanrevolution.com, where there is a link to a downloadable spreadsheet that has a list of the firemen of 1776 with their military units.

319. *COHM*, 1:233, 317.

320. *NYRCS*, 1:15.

321. Wright, *Continental Army*, 93; U.S. Army Center of Military History, "Chapter 5: An Army for the War: 1777," www.history.army.mil; John A. Tures, "More Americans Fought in the American Revolution than We Thought," *Observer*, July 3, 2017, www.observer.com; *Encyclopedia of the American Revolution* (Boatner) estimates that there were 375,000 men in the armed forces, which is about 15 percent of the population listed in *Continental Army* (Wright).
322. Wright, *Continental Army*, 98.
323. *COHM*, 1:27.
324. *NYRCS*, 1:155–57 (Stoutenburgh at the Second [1775–76]/Third Provincial Congress [1776]).
325. Burrows and Wallace, *Gotham*, 245.
326. "Proclamation by Major General James Robertson," *NYG-WM*, no. 1,316 (January 13, 1777): 3; Stokes, *Iconography*, 5:1,044.
327. "New-York, August 10," *NYG-WM*, no. 1,399 (August 10, 1778): 3.
328. Stokes, *Iconography*, 5:1,072.
329. Ibid.
330. Manuscript provided by the New York City Fire Museum from a private collection.
331. "New-York, August 17," *Royal Gazette*, no. 615 (August 17, 1782): 3.
332. "Manifesto," *NYG-WM*, no. 1,414 (November 23, 1778): 1.
333. "Fire Buckets," *Royal Gazette*, no. 437 (December 6, 1780): 2.
334. "Tickets," *NYG-WM*, no. 1,493 (May 29, 1780): 4.
335. "General Account," *NYG-WM*, no. 1,598 (June 3, 1782): 3. This assumes the typographical error in the newspaper for the rent credits of £35,000 was actually £45,000, which would have balanced the balance sheet. When reported by the collector/treasurer, the yield from the lotteries for the period of 1777–82 was given in pounds as £10,000 18s 4p.
336. "General Account," *NYG-WM*, no. 1,598 (June 3, 1782): 3. The £4,261 line item for fire engines, et cetera, was more than enough to cover building new engines. Stanton, one of the Loyalist firemen— and previously an assistant engineer under Stoutenburgh—had built engines for the department as recently as 1774. The most recent engines cost less than £100 (for example, one for £90 and another smaller engine was £50).
337. "Proclamation by Major General James Robertson," *NYG-WM*, no. 1,316 (January 13, 1777): 3.
338. Stokes, *Iconography*, 5:1,08.
339. "By Samuel Birch, Esq.," *Royal Gazette*, no. 434 (November 25, 1780): 4.

340. "New-York, March 8," *Royal Gazette*, no. 359 (March 8, 1780): 3.

341. Stokes, *Iconography*, 5:1,104.

342. Costello, *Our Firemen*, 585–90.

343. Ibid., 585; See also appendix 20 on www.savingny.com with spreadsheets containing the names in each fire company by engine and year.

344. "Whereas There Are a Number of Firemen," *NYG-WM*, no. 1,660 (August 11, 1783): 3.

345. Burrows and Wallace, *Gotham*, 258.

346. See "Illustration 30: Proposal for a Post-War Fire Department," Saving New York, www.savingny.com, for the complete petition. See also, Costello, *Our Firemen*, 42–44.

347. *Independent New-York Gazette*, Saturday, December 6, 1783, no. 3, 4.

348. Comparing the list of foremen in Costello's facsimile of the engineers' letter to Clinton with the roster as printed in the *MCCCNY* in 1772.

349. *MCCCNY*, 8:5.

350. Sixty of the firefighters from the 1772 and 1776 lists were also on the lists in 1783 and 1786. For the 1786 list, see *MCCCNY-2*, 1:200–3 (fire department of February 15, 1786).

351. Burrows and Wallace, *Gotham*, 245, 258; United States Census Bureau, "Population."

Epilogue

352. *MCCCNY-2*, 1:82.

353. Last will and testament of Jacobus Stoutenburgh, December 4, 1772, probated June 12, 1784.

354. *NYRCS*, 2:155–57. Also see Wikipedia, www.en.wikipedia.org.

355. *NYRCS*, 2:260–61.

356. *MCCCNY-2*, 8:490, 9:184.

357. Ibid., 8:546.

358. Ibid., 9:418, 11:131; Barrett, *Old Merchants*, 342.

REFERENCES FOR ILLUSTRATIONS

*T*he illustrations in *New York Firefighting and the American Revolution*, except for those noted below (with an asterisk), are original or, in the case of maps, redrafts or composites of seventeenth- and eighteenth-century canonical maps. The originals were illustrated by Devan Calabrez in collaboration with Bruce Twickler for Docema LLC, all rights reserved, and appear here courtesy of Docema LLC.

See Saving New York (www.savingny.com) for extended references and analyses and supplemental views of original illustrations.

Introduction

Newsworthy Fires (1766–1775): see www.savingny.com/appendix19 for links to newspaper accounts of fires.

Explosives Discovered at the 1776 Fire: see www.savingny.com/appendix25 for a list of sworn witnesses.

Part One

Mill near the fort: see www.savingny.com/newamsterdam for other views of New Amsterdam.

Exchange Rate of Guilders and Pelts: see www.savingny.com/appendix3 for extended currency analysis.

The Colony of New Netherland: an original Docema map overlaying modern satellite photographs.

Colonial Dutch house: see www.savingny.com/roelantsen for other views of the Roelantsen house.

1650 wood frame: see www.savingny.com/roelantsen for other views of the Roelantsen house.

Two-thousand-foot-long defensive wall: original artistic conception based on specifications in *The Records of New Amsterdam* (Fernow), see www.savingny.com/appendix5.

1653 plank wall: original, as specified in *The Records of New Amsterdam* (Fernow), see www.savingny.com/appendix5.

1660 Map of Wall: redraft of the Castello Map, as discussed at www.savingny.com/maps1658.

Bucket brigade: what the crew of the spaceship USS *Enterprise* would look like in an eighteenth-century bucket brigade.

English warships: see www.savingny.com/newamsterdam for other views of New Amsterdam.

1700 Map of Wards: a composite of Stokes/Miller maps, see www.savingny.com/maps1695.

1703 New York Census: see www.savingny.com/maps1695 for a complete 1703 census and spreadsheet analysis.

Dutch to English Ethnic Shift: data from Joyce D. Goodfriend (*Before the Melting Pot*), pages 62 and 156–57.

*London Broadside, circa 1730 (partial): see the full page at www.savingny.com/appendix13.html#broadside.

1725 Newsham fire engine: see www.savingny.com/newsham for more views of the engine and references

X-ray engine views: see www.savingny.com/newsham for more views of the engine.

Part Two

The Newsham Engine: see www.savingny.com/newsham for more views of the engine, including "X-rays."

*Mid-eighteenth-century firefighting (partial): see a complete engraving at www.savingny.com.

*Advanced Dutch firefighting: Jan van der Heyden (1637–1712). *Beschryving der Nieuwlyks Uitgevonden en Geoctrojeerde Slang-Brand-Spuiten En Haare Wyze Van Brand-Blussen (Description of the Newly Discovered and Patented Hose Fire Engine and Its Way of Extinguishing Fires)*. Amsterdam: Jan Rieuwertsz, 1690. See other van der Heyden images at www.savingny.com/appendix10.

1741 Fires: see www.savingny.com/maps1741 for reference maps and data links.

1769 Map of Wards and Engines: see www.savingny.com/appendix17 for reference maps and data links.

Funding for the Night Watch: see www.savingny.com/appendix16 for a spreadsheet analysis of expenditures.

The Growth of the FDNY: see www.savingny.com/appendix18 for an increase in number of engines and firefighters.

Newsworthy Fires by Category: see www.savingny.com/appendix19 for links to newspaper accounts of fires.

FDNY Before the Revolution: see www.savingny.com/appendix21 for lists of firemen from 1772 and 1776.

*Colonists favoring imports (partial): *new-York Gazette*, or *Weekly Post-Boy*, no. 1,438 (July 23, 1770). See all pages at www.savingny.com/appendix20.

*1776 list of firemen (partial): *Calendar of Historical Manuscripts Relating to the War of Revolution* 1: 315, 316. See both pages at www.savingny.com/appendix21.

FDNY in the Revolution: see www.savingny.com/appendix22 for estimates of where firemen were from 1776 to 1783.

Part Three

View from Wall Street and Broadway: original illustration from a Docema 3D model, see www.savingny.com/appendix24.html for references.

Great Fire of 1776 Begins: see www.savingny.com/maps1776 for references of this and other 1776 fire maps.

The 1776 Fire, 12:00 to 2:00 a.m.: see www.savingny.com/maps1776 for references.

The FDNY at the Exchange: original, see www.savingny.com for reference images.

The Fire, 2:00 to 4:00 a.m.: see www.savingny.com/maps1776 for references.

The Fire, after 4:00 a.m.: see www.savingny.com/maps1776 for references.

*The Sugar House: Miriam and Ira D. Wallach Division of Art, Prints and Photographs: Print Collection, New York Public Library. "Van Cortlandt's Sugar House." New York Public Library Digital Collections. www.digitalcollections.nypl.org.

The FDNY at St. Paul's: see the original illustration and find reference images at www.savingny.com.

The Fire ends at King's College: original, see www.savingny.com for reference images.

Trinity Church before the fire: original, see www.savingny.com/appendix24 for reference images.

Trinity Church after the fire: original, see www.savingny.com/appendix24 for reference images.

Combustible Explosives: see www.savingny.com/appendix25 for a list of sworn witnesses.

The 1783 Carleton Commission: see www.savingny.com/carletonhighlights for more details.

The 1778 Fire: see www.savingny.com/appendix27 for references and a review of previous maps.

Revolutionary Fires: see www.savingny.com/appendix28 for references.

*1783 advertisement for firemen: *New-York Gazette* and *Weekly Mercury Monday*, no. 1,660 (August 11, 1783): 3.

*1783 Loyalist proposal (partial): a facsimile of the letter published in Costello, *Our Firemen: A History of the New York Fire Departments, Volunteer and Paid* (1887). See the complete letter at www.savingny.com/illustration30.

ADDITIONAL REFERENCES

Manhattan, August 1664: see www.savingny.com/newamsterdam for other views of New Amsterdam.

*Isaac Stoutenburgh (partial): see the Stoutenburgh-Teller website for a genealogy of the Stoutenburghs and a full image (www.stoutenburgh-teller.com/colonial-portrait-isaac-stoutenburgh).

*Marinus Willett (partial): see the Metropolitan Museum of Art's website for a full image and the context of this portrait (www.metmuseum.org/art/collection/search/10833).

*John Jay (partial): see the National Gallery for a full image and context (www.npg.si.edu/object/npg_NPG.74.46).

BIBLIOGRAPHY

Abbreviations for References

CCR
Board of Enquiry Into the Cause of the Great Fire in the City of New York in September 1776. Recorded by Ward Chipman. New York: New-York Historical Society, 1776–80, misc. MSS boxes 12 and 13. (Hereafter referred to as the "Carleton Commission Report.")

CLONY
The Colonial Laws of New York. Albany: James D. Lyon, state printer, 1894.

COHM
Calendar of Historical Manuscripts Relating to the War of Revolution. Albany: Weed, Parsons and Company, 1868.

DRCH
Documents Relative to the Colonial History of the State of New York. Vols. 1–11, Edited/translated by E.B. O'Callaghan; vols. 12–15, edited and translated by B. Fernow. John Romyn Brodhead, agent. Albany, NY: Weed, Parsons and Company, printers, 1858.

JOPC
Journal of the Provincial Congress. Albany, NY: Thurlow Weed, printer to the state, 1842.

MCCCNY
Minutes of the Common Council of the City of New York 1675–1776. New York: Dodd, Mead and Company, 1905.

MCCCNY-2
Minutes of the Common Council of the City of New York 1784–1831. New York: City of New York, 1917.

NYIR
New York in the Revolution. James A. Roberts, comptroller (ed.). Albany, NY: Brandow Printing Company, 1898.

NYRCS
Office of State Comptroller. *New York in the Revolution as a Colony and State.* Albany, NY: J.B. Lyon Company, 1904.

ABBREVIATIONS FOR NEWSPAPERS

NYG
New-York Gazette (1725–44) (1759–67)

NYG-P
New-York Gazette, or Weekly Post-Boy

NYG-WM
New-York Gazette, and Weekly Mercury (1768–83)

NYJ
New-York Journal (1733–51)

NYM
New-York Mercury (1752–68)

SOURCES

Anderson, Fred. *The Crucible of War.* New York: Alfred A. Knopf, 2000.

Aptheker, Herbert. *American Negro Slave Revolts.* New York: International Publishers, 1993.

Archdeacon, Thomas J. *New York City, 1674–1710: Conquest and Change.* Ithaca, NY: Cornell University Press, 1976.

Atkinson, Rick. *The British Are Coming: The War for America, Lexington to Princeton 1775–1777.* The Revolution Trilogy. New York: Henry Holt and Co., 1999.

Bakeless, John. *Turncoats, Traitors and Heroes.* New York: De Capo Press, 1998.

Barrett, Walter. *The Old Merchants of New York City.* New York: Geo. W. Carleton, 1863.

Becker, Carl. *The Eve of Revolution.* New Haven, CT: Yale University Press, 1918.

————. *The History of Political Parties in the Province of New York.* Reprinted from the Bulletin of the University of Wisconsin History Series, vol. 2. Madison: University of Wisconsin, 1909.

Boatner, Mark M. *Encyclopedia of the American Revolution.* Reprint, Mechanicksburg, PA: Stackpole Books, 1994.

Braidwood, James. *Fire Prevention and Fire Extinction.* London: Bell and Daldy, 1866.

Brayley, A.W. *A Complete History of the Boston Fire Department.* Boston: John P. Dale & Co., 1889.

Brindenbaugh, Carl. *Cities in the Wilderness.* New York: Capricorn Books, 1964.

Burrows, Edward G., and Mike Wallace. *Gotham: A History of New York City to 1898.* Oxford: Oxford University Press, 1999.

Burrows, Edwin. *Forgotten Patriots: The Untold Story of American Prisoners During the Revolutionary War.* New York: Basic Books, 2008.

Cannon, Donald J., ed. *Heritage of Flames.* New York: Doubleday and Company Inc., 1977.

Carp, Benjamin L. "The Night the Yankees Burned Broadway: The New York City Fire of 1776." *Early American Studies* 4, no. 2 (2006): 471–511.

Costello, Augustine E. *Our Firemen: A History of the New York Fire Departments, Volunteer and Paid.* 1887. Reprint, New York: Knickerbocker Press, 1997.

Dana, David D. *The Firemen: The Fire Departments of the United States.* Boston: James French and Company, 1858.

Dawson, Henry B. "Incidents in the History of the Volunteer Fire Department of New York 1648–1783." Vol. 6. MSS at the New-York Historical Society, AHMC.

Edwards, George William. *New York as an Eighteenth-Century Municipality.* New York: Columbia University Press, 1917.

Fernow, Berthold, ed. *The Records of New Amsterdam from 1653 to 1674 Anno Domini.* New York: Knickerbocker Press, 1897.

Force, Peter. *American Archives.* Washington, D.C.: Clarke and Force, 1851.

Fox, Frank L. *A Distant Storm.* Rotherfield, UK: Jean Boudriot Publications, 1996.

———. *The Four Days Battle of 1666.* Andover, MA: Docema LLC, 2009.

———. *Great Ships: The Battlefleet of King Charles II.* London: Conway Maritime Press, 1980.

Franklin, Benjamin. *The Papers of Benjamin Franklin.* Edited by Ellen R. Cohn. New Haven, CT: Yale University Press, 2011.

———. *The Papers of Benjamin Franklin.* Edited by Leonard W. Labaree. New Haven, CT: Yale University Press, 1963.

Gaine, Hugh. Publisher/Editorials. *New-York Gazette* and the *Weekly Mercury,* 1768–83.

Goodfriend, Joyce D. *Before the Melting Pot.* Princeton, NJ: Princeton University Press, 1992.

Grim, David. *Collections of the New-York Historical Society for the Year 1870.* New York: Printed for the society, 1871.

Grizzard, Frank E., Jr., and David R. Hoth, eds. *The Papers of George Washington: Revolutionary War Series.* Charlottesville: University Press of Virginia, 2002. www.rotunda.upress.virginia.edu.

Hafner, Donald. L. *William Smith, Captain.* Lincoln, MA: Lincoln Historical Society, 2017.

Hanson, Neil. *The Great Fire of London: In that Apocalyptic Year, 1666.* Hoboken, NJ: John Wiley & Sons, 2002.

Harding, Richard. *Seapower and Naval Warfare 1650–1830.* Annapolis, MD: Naval Institute Press, 1999.

Heath, William (major general). *Heath's Memoirs of the American War.* New York: A. Wessels Company, 1904.

Henry, John Joseph. *Campaign Against Quebec.* Watertown, NY: Knowlton and Rice, 1844.

Horsmanden, Daniel. *A Journal of the Proceedings in the Detection of the Conspiracy Formed by Some White People, in Conjunction with Negro and other Slaves, for Burning the City of New-York in America, and Murdering the Inhabitants.* New York: James Parker, 1744.

———. *The New-York Conspiracy or History of the Negro Plot, with the Journal of the Proceedings Against the Conspirators at New York in the Years 1741–2.* New York: Southwick and Pelsue, 1810.

Hough, Franklin. *Census of the State of New-York, for 1855*. Albany, NY: Charles Van Benthuysen, 1858.

Howe, Richard. "Material City." Unpublished correspondence.

Ingram, Arthur. *A History of Firefighting and Equipment*. Seacaucus, NJ: Chartwell Books, 1978.

Israel, Jonathan. *The Dutch Republic*. New York: Clarendon Press, 1998.

Jacobs, Jaap. "The Early Years of Peter Stuyvesant." In *Revisiting New Netherland*. Edited by Joyce D. Goodfriend. Boston: Brill Publishers, 2005.
———. *New Netherland: A Dutch Colony in Seventeenth-Century America*. Boston: Brill Publishers, 2005.

Jones, Thomas. *The History of New York During the Revolutionary War*. Edited by Edward Floyd de Lancey. New York: Printed for the New York Historical Society, 1879.

Kessler, Henry K., and Eugen Rachlis. *Peter Stuyvesant and His New York*. New York: Random House, 1959.

Knight, Sarah Kemble. *The Private Journal of a Journey from Boston to New York in the Year 1704*. Albany, NY: Frank H. Little, 1865.

Lepore, Jill. *New York Burning: Liberty, Slavery, and Conspiracy in Eighteenth-Century Manhattan*. New York: Vintage, 2007.

Limpus, Lowell M. *History of the New York Fire Department*. New York: E.P. Dutton and Company Inc., 1940.

Mackenzie, Frederick. *Diary of Frederick Mackenzie: Giving a Daily Narrative of His Military Service as an Officer of the Regiment of Royal Welch Fusiliers During the Years 1775–1781*. Cambridge, MA: Harvard University Press, 1930.

Maika, Dennis J. "Commerce and Community: Manhattan Merchants in the Seventeenth Century." PhD diss., New York University, 1995.

Martinoli, Beverly Marion (Paine). *The Paine-French Genealogy*. Bloomington, IN: Trafford Publishing, 2011.

McCullough, David. *1776*. New York: Simon and Schuster, 2005.

Molhuysen, P.C., and P.J. Blok. *Nieuw Nederlansch Biografisch Woordenboek*. Leiden: A.W. Sijthoffs, 1911.

Moore, Frank. *Diary of the American Revolution*. New York: Charles Scribner, 1860.

Multhauf, Leslie Stibbe. *Van Der Heyden: A Description of Fire Engines with Water Hoses and the Method of Fighting Fires Now Used in Amsterdam*. Canton, MA: Science History Publications, 1996.

New York City During the Revolution. New York: Mercantile Library Association of New York City, 1861.

New York Historical Manuscripts. Vol. 2. Register of the Provincial Secretary, 1642–1647. Dutch translated and annotated by Arnold J.F. Van Laer. Edited by Kenneth Scott and Kenn Stryker-Rodda. Baltimore, MD: Genealogical Publishing Co. Inc., 1974.

O'Callaghan, E.B. *Register of New Netherlands.* Albany, NY: J. Munsell, 1765.

Peña, Elizabeth Shapiro. "Wampum Production in New Netherland and New York: The Historical and Archeological Context." PhD diss., Boston University, 1990.

Peterson, Arthur Everett. "New York as an Eighteenth Century Municipality: Prior to 1731." PhD diss., Columbia University, New York, 1917.

Pincus, Steven. *Protestantism and Patriotism.* Cambridge: Cambridge University Press, 1996.

Rabin, Serena R., ed. *The New York Conspiracy Trials of 1741.* Boston: Bedford/St. Martin's, 2004.

Rink, Oliver A. *Holland on the Hudson: An Economic and Social History of Dutch New York.* Ithaca, NY: Cornell, 1986.

Ritchie, Robert C. *The Duke's Province: A Study of New York Politics and Society, 1664–1691.* Chapel Hill: University of North Carolina Press, 1977.

Russell, J. Franklin, ed. *Narratives of New Netherland 1609–1664.* Reprint, New York: Barnes and Noble, 1967.

Schecter, Barnet. *The Battle for New York: The City at the Heart of the American Revolution.* New York: Walker and Co., 2002.

Schomette, Donald G., and Robert D. Haslach. *Raid on America: The Dutch Naval Campaign of 1672–1674.* Columbia: University of South Carolina Press, 1988.

Schultz, Eric B., and Michael J. Tougias. *King Philip's War: The History and Legacy of America's Forgotten Conflict.* New York: Countryman Press, 1999.

Scott, Kenneth, and Kenn Stryker-Roda. *Denizations, Naturalizations, and Oaths of Allegiance in Colonial New York.* Baltimore, MD: Genealogical Publishing Co., 1975.

Shelton, William Henry. *The Jumel Mansion.* New York: Houghton Mifflin, 1916.

Sheppard, Frances. *London: A History.* New York: Oxford University Press, 1998.

Shorto, Russell. *The Island at the Center of the World.* New York: Doubleday, 2004.

Spence, Craig. *Accidents and Violent Death in Early Modern London, 1650–1750.* Woodbridge, UK: Boydell & Brewer, 2016.

Stokes, I.N. Phelps. *Iconography of Manhattan Island.* 6 vols. New York: Robert Dodd, 1915–26.

Stone, William L. *History: New York City.* New York: E. Cleave, 1868.

Sutton, Peter C. *Jan van der Heyden (1637–1712).* New Haven, CT: Yale University Press, 2006.

Switzer, Stephen. *An Introduction to a General System of Hydrostaticks and Hydraulics.* London: T. Astley and L. Gilliver, 1729.

Van Buskirk, Judith. *Generous Enemies.* Philadelphia: University of Pennsylvania Press, 2002.

Van Der Heyden, Jan. *Slang Brand Spuiten.* Amsterdam: Jan Rieuwertsz, 1690.

Washington, George. *The Papers of George Washington, Revolutionary War Series.* Edited by Philander D. Chase and Frank E. Grizzard Jr. Charlottesville: University Press of Virginia, 1994.

Woodcroft, Bennet. *Appendix to Reference Index of Patents of Invention.* London: Commissioners of Patents/Great Seal Patent Office, 1855.

Wright, Robert K. *The Continental Army.* Washington, D.C.: Center of Military History, United States Army, 1983.

ABOUT THE AUTHOR

 ruce Twickler also produced, wrote and directed the acclaimed PBS documentaries *Damrell's Fire* (2006) and *Broadside* (2009). Before becoming a filmmaker, Twickler published animation and video software—VideoWorks (1985) and VideoCraft (1995)—and founded an internet company, Andover.net (IPO, 1999). Before publishing, he cofounded a chain of retail Hi-Fi stores and worked as a research engineer at MITRE Corp after receiving his BS/MSEE from MIT. He now lives with his wife on Cape Cod and often visits his grown kids and rapidly growing grandkids.